Wake Up with Purpose!

Wake Up with Purpose!

What I've Learned in My First Hundred Years

Sister Jean Dolores Schmidt, BVM

with Seth Davis

Harper Select

Wake Up with Purpose!

Copyright © 2023 by Jean Dolores Schmidt, BVM ("Sister Jean")

Published by Harper Select, an imprint of HarperCollins Focus LLC.

Published in association with David Black Literary Agency, 355 Adams Street, Suite 2707, Brooklyn, NY 11201.

Any internet addresses, phone numbers, or company or product information printed in this book are offered as a resource and are not intended in any way to be or to imply an endorsement by Harper Focus, nor does Harper Focus vouch for the existence, content, or services of these sites, phone numbers, companies, or products beyond the life of this book.

ISBN 978-1-4003-3351-6 (HC)
ISBN 978-1-4003-3357-8 (Ebook)
ISBN 978-1-4003-3358-5 (Audio)

Library of Congress Cataloging-in-Publication Data on File

Printed in the United States of America
23 24 25 26 27 LBC 6 5 4 3 2

Contents

Contents

Prologue

At my age I'm always happy when I wake up.

MY ALARM CLOCK GOES off each morning at 5 a.m. It takes me a couple of seconds to shake off the cobwebs. Then I sit up quickly. If I don't, I might fall back to sleep. Can't let that happen—I've got too much to do.

First, though, I say a prayer. I put my feet on the floor and sit on the edge of my bed. *Oh, God, thank You for bringing me this day and for letting me serve You once again.* I then get myself cleaned and dressed and into my wheelchair. I don't use the chair because I'm old. I broke my hip, and then I got shingles. I am hoping the chair is only temporary, but I'm not complaining. I know I'm blessed to have the chair and the ability to move those wheels, as well as plenty of people who are willing to push me around.

Now that I'm clean and settled, I can begin my daily thirty-minute morning meditation. I take out my iPad and open an application from the US Conference of Catholic Bishops, where I study my gospel reading for the day. I guess there aren't too many 103-year-old nuns using iPads these days—there aren't too many 103-year-old people, *period*—but I'm pretty comfortable with modern technology. I've always said, if you're not moving forward, you're going to get left behind real quick. Adaptability is my superpower.

I actually think the iPad is a wonderful way to absorb Scripture. It's light and fits easily into my hands. Beside each reading is a reflection from a theologian, which encapsulates that day's section, so I indulge in that text too. It gives me a deeper understanding and appreciation as I read the ancient words.

My reading done, I sit and reflect. When I was studying to be a sister, I learned to set aside time each day to sit quietly and think. Now, if I notice I'm distracted, which is natural, I try to get myself back to God. When you have so much on your mind, it's easy to be distracted. We're human beings, after all.

Finally, I set aside the iPad and look out the window of my apartment at The Clare, an assisted living facility for senior citizens in downtown Chicago. The city is so peaceful at this early hour. There's a hotel across the street, and I see lights in the rooms start to come on. I think about the people waking up in those rooms, and I pray that they will find joy on this day the Lord has made. I can see a corner of Lake Michigan peeking out from behind the hotel. I call that my piece of the lake. Sometimes, when the water is nice and calm, I can see sailboats out there. I think about those people on the boats and pray that they will be safe and enjoy their time on the water.

As I continue to pray and meditate, I consider my work for the day. I go over my schedule so I know what I have to look forward to. I try to be as specific as I can at the start, even though I know not everything will go according to what I've laid out. I reflect on what's going to be good about the day ahead, as well as what I'm not looking forward to. That's okay, though, because I know whatever problems come up, they will get resolved. I trust that God has His plan in place. This adjusts my mindset for the day.

I think we could all be a little happier and more productive if we set aside quiet time, especially at the start of our days. Even five or ten minutes of silent reflection can be enough. I did this for many years as an eighth-grade teacher. I would begin class by asking my students to put their heads down on their desks while I read from the gospel. This calmed them down. At first I did this for five minutes. Eventually I extended it to ten. Then at the end of class we would sit quietly for a few additional minutes so everyone could think about what had been read.

Saint Ignatius of Loyola, the fifteenth-century Spanish priest who founded the religious order of the Society of Jesus, also known as the Jesuits, was a great advocate for quiet. He devised a daily Examen prayer to be said during the course of the day. The Examen provides for silent reflections on thanksgiving, petition, review, response, and a prayer for tomorrow. Today millions of Catholics around the world say their Examen at least once a day. There are few rituals that bring me more peace.

Perhaps my favorite place to pray is Madonna della Strada Chapel on Loyola's campus. It is a quiet place that is conducive to prayer. Even though many visitors come and go, I experience quiet alone time with God, and I believe that He listens to me as I talk to Him about my friends, my activities, and what I hope to do in my ministry at Loyola.

Other times I like to sit by the lake and enjoy the beauties that

God has created and shared with all of us. I thank Him for such gifts.

Along with that time for reflection, I also understand we all need a pat on the back once in a while, including from ourselves. Before I go to sleep each night, I think of all the good things I did that day. That way I know I will wake up happy in the morning. Although, let's face it, at my age I'm always happy when I wake up. And when I do, I sit up and start my morning ritual all over again, awash in gratitude that once again God has empowered me to wake up with purpose.

When I turned one hundred years old on August 21, 2019, the city of Chicago and my employer, Loyola University, threw a big party for me. There's nothing I enjoy more than a big party, especially when I'm the guest of honor! One of the local reporters asked our former basketball coach, Porter Moser, how I'd lived so long and so happily. "Well, I'll tell you," he replied. "She has a purpose every day."

I think there's a lot of truth to that. Of course, there's also a lot of luck involved in living this long. I'm extremely blessed that I've never gotten terribly sick or badly hurt. I've also clearly inherited great DNA. My father lived until he was ninety-five and my two brothers lived until they were seventy-four and ninety years old. I do think having a daily, consistent purpose has kept me not only alive but young and vibrant.

I've always loved my work because it never feels like work. To this day, I report for work at Loyola University Chicago five days a week. My office sits right in the heart of our student center, so those magnificent young people are constantly popping in and out of my office to ask questions, say hello, or request a selfie. I am the *queen* of the selfie these days. My evenings are filled with phone calls, reading, and writing emails. (Yes, I write my own emails.) I'd like to think that I've got just as much, if not more, energy as people who are many years my junior. I only wish I could jump out of this wheelchair and dance a jig!

I can't say I planned to live this long, or decided a course of action that would allow it to happen. I just followed my instincts— and my calling to serve God. This intention first popped into my head when I was a third grader attending Catholic school in San Francisco. My teacher was a Sister of Charity of the Blessed Virgin Mary, and I announced that I wanted to be just like her. I never looked back. I was eighteen years old when I entered the BVM motherhouse in 1937, and I have been an educator ever since. For the first twenty years of my career, I taught in elementary school, mostly in my native California. When I started I taught fifth grade, and later moved to eighth grade. Besides being a teacher, I was also an administrator, principal, and basketball coach, as well as coaching other sports. In 1961, I moved to Mundelein College, an all-women's college in Chicago. Thirty years after that, Mundelein affiliated with Loyola University. I have worked there ever since.

I've had many duties at Loyola over the last three decades, but few have brought me more joy than my service as the chaplain for the men's basketball team. I meet with the team before every game to offer a team prayer. I also pray with the fans shortly before tip-off. Then I watch the action from my wheelchair right next to the court. From where I sit, I can see everything that happens, including all the instances when the referees make a bad call—and I pray that those guys will get better eyesight. Sometimes, the players will stop and hug me on their way off the court. There's nothing like hugging a sweaty basketball player after a big win.

I may be an old nun, but I know my hoops. On the day after each game, I send emails to the coaches and players offering my analysis of the game and a scouting report for our upcoming opponent. I know basketball well, having watched it all these years, and I make sure to do my homework. Then, before the next game, we meet again, and I pray for everyone to be safe and healthy—and for the Ramblers to win.

I often see looks of surprise on the guys' faces when they hear some of the things I say. One of our players, Donte Ingram, once told a reporter how surprised he was when he heard me deliver a pregame prayer for the first time.

"It caught me off guard," he said. "I thought she was just going to pray. She prayed, but then she starts saying, 'You've got to box out and watch out for number 23.'"

I've been blessed to be well-known in the Loyola community for quite some time, but in the spring of 2018 I reached a level of notoriety that I never could have imagined when my Ramblers made a Cinderella run to the Final Four of the NCAA tournament. Every time we took the court, we were the underdogs, but our guys showed such great fight and teamwork that we were able to win four straight games. As they took each step, the press developed a bigger fascination with the old nun in the wheelchair wearing a maroon and gold scarf and a pair of Nike sneakers with the words "Sister" and "Jean" stitched onto them.

By the time we all arrived in San Antonio for the Final Four, I was such a big deal that the NCAA set up my own press conference.

Prologue

They told me afterward I drew more reporters than Tom Brady did at the Super Bowl. At one point, a reporter asked how it felt to be a national celebrity. *"International* celebrity," I corrected. That's because I had received emails from Europe from friends who had caught wind of my story across the pond. This nun was flying.

The tournament ended for us with a loss to Michigan in the Final Four. I was disappointed, of course, but I was so thrilled for what those players and coaches had accomplished. Life has calmed down for me in the years since then—but only a little. I am still treated like a celebrity, and I must say I do enjoy it because it gives me the chance to interact with so many people. People tease me from time to time—"Now, Sister Jean, don't let this go to your head"—but of course it hasn't. I believe this was all a part of God's plan.

All I ever wanted to do was serve God, and my way of doing that has been to work with young people to educate them, encourage them, give them spiritual guidance, and help them live out their dreams. I have seen so many changes over the last century, but the important things have remained the same.

My attitude and perspective haven't changed since Loyola's amazing run to the Final Four, but I recognize that I have a much bigger audience now. I feel it is my duty to take advantage of this holy opportunity. That is my aim in writing this book—not just to tell the story of my life but also to talk about all the things I learned during my first hundred years. I hope to do what I've always done: use my words to help others learn, grow, serve God, and serve one another. I hope when people read this book, they will be able to wake up the way I do. I want them to wake up happy. I want them to wake up with purpose.

And I want the Ramblers to win.

One

It Starts with Belief

If you keep your faith, you never have to grow old.

I RECENTLY CAME UPON an African proverb that said, "When an old person dies, a library closes." I thought that was such a beautiful verse. And by that logic, if the old person is still living, that means the library is open, right?

That's a pleasant way to imagine myself. I'd like to think I have information to share and stories to tell that could be helpful and inspirational to others. And you don't need a library card to hear my stories. All you have to do is pull up a chair and ask. As someone who was born just nine months after World War I, I've seen a great deal.

My earliest memory stretches back to when I was two and a half years old. It was April of 1922, and my grandmother had just died. My brother Ed had been born that January, and several days before the funeral, he came down with a bad case of whooping cough. He had caught it from me, and my mother was concerned because babies have a hard time getting rid of phlegm. I distinctly remember being at the cemetery and seeing someone bring a folding chair for my mother so she didn't have to stand while holding the baby.

The next day, my brother stopped coughing. My mother told me it was because Grandma had cured him.

This was how it was for our family. Everything started with belief. Although I was sad that my grandma had died, my mother encouraged me by telling me Grandma was already with God in heaven and was helping to keep us safe and healthy.

My dad taught us that God made the stars and the skies, and that He loved us, He was always watching over us, and He wanted us to be happy. Of course, that doesn't mean that everything will go our way, but if we hold on to that belief, we can trust that God has a reason for everything that happens, even if we don't quite understand it at the time.

That's an easy concept to grasp when you're two and a half years old. But it gets harder to understand as we get older. It's like what is said about the angel Clarence at the beginning of the classic Christmas movie *It's a Wonderful Life*: "He's got the faith of a child." Wouldn't it be nice if someone could always say that about us? That's why every day of my life, I've sought to reaffirm my belief and reestablish my faith. That's how it works with God. If you keep your faith, you never have to grow old.

I've always had a pretty good memory—almost too good. When I was in first grade I didn't read books so much as memorize them. If I had to read in front of the class, I would purposely hold the book upside down to show off to my fellow students that I wasn't actually reading it. Yup, I was kind of a ham, even back then. My father was none too pleased when he discovered this. He made sure I learned to read well.

My mother grew up as the daughter of devout Catholics. She didn't like her first name, Bertha—maybe it's because there was a famous lady at the circus named Bertha who was known for her substantial girth, but I guess her parents weren't aware of that. She preferred to be called Bert. When she was a little girl, she decided she wanted to marry a man whose name was Joseph, because that was the foster father of Jesus. Later on, her older brothers started working in San Francisco for a Catholic magazine, and they met a young man who worked there whose name was Joseph. They set up a date, but my mother decided this was not the right Joseph for her. However, on the second date, she changed her mind. (You may want to keep that in mind the next time you have a so-so first date.)

They settled in the Bay Area of California. I was their firstborn, coming into the world on August 21, 1919. They named me Dolores Bertha. Two and a half years later, my brother Ed arrived. Four years after him came Raymond. Our grandfather lived with us as well. I thought sometimes this must have been tough on my parents, but I'm sure it was nice for them to have an extra babysitter.

It's a Catholic tradition in my mother's native region of Alsace-Lorraine that after a child is born, the mother takes the baby to a church to be dedicated to the Blessed Virgin Mary. The ritual dictates that the mother has to wait until forty days after the baby is born so she's "clean" again. My mother performed this ritual with me and my brothers. Another part of the tradition is that the child is supposed to wear blue for the first seven years if it's a daughter and for three years if it's a son. I used to wear baby bonnets with roses on them, and my mother had to switch them all out for blue ones. My mother often said she changed more roses on my bonnets than she had time for.

Both my parents came from big families. My mother had three sisters and two brothers, although her mother lost several other children at birth. My father had six sisters and two brothers, as well as a third brother who died when he was twenty-one. My father was the only one of his siblings who got married and had children. All of his brothers and sisters lived in the same house. They all worked except one sister, to whom they paid a salary to stay home and do all the cooking and cleaning.

The upshot of all this is that my brothers and I had many uncles and aunts but very few cousins. How spoiled we were! The family would come over to our house and dote on us, or we would go to their house and be the object of all their affections.

Even though my grandpa lived with us, I was put in charge of my brothers a lot. I often tried to boss them around, but they also let me play with them and their friends. A big reason my brothers and I got along so well was that we never tattled on one another. If our parents asked us what was happening, we told them the truth, but if something went wrong between us, we took care of it ourselves. I felt responsible for Ed and Raymond and didn't want them to get into trouble, although it happened from time to time. For instance, one day a few older boys in town asked Ed, "Do you like fire engines?" He was four years old, so of course he said yes. They told him, "Well, if you pull the little button on that telephone pole over there, we'll see a lot of fire engines."

This made him very excited. A boy lifted up Ed, and he pulled the lever. Sure enough, the fire engines came blaring. When they did, the other boys ran away. My brother got scared and ran home and crawled under the kitchen table. When my mother found him, he told her what had happened.

Our doorbell rang and my mother opened the door to see a fireman standing there holding a little black book. He came inside, sat down, listened to my brother tell his story, and jotted notes. He was very nice but stern. "If this happens again," he said to my brother, "we will have to come back and have a different kind of conversation. Do you understand?" Those firemen never had to come back, that was for sure.

There was only one time I remember when I got in real trouble with my parents. I got mad at my brother and kicked him. I didn't mean to hurt him, but it landed right on his shin and he started bleeding. My mom talked to me about it, but she wasn't much for punishments. She would rather reason with us and let us think about what was right or wrong based on our conversation.

There was another time when my brother Ed was five years old and he asked my mother if he could do something. When she said no, he called her an SOB. She took him into the bathroom, grabbed a bar of lavender soap, and washed his mouth with it. He started crying, which only created more soap bubbles. When it was over, Mom said to him gently, "Now will you ever do that again?" He promised he wouldn't, and as far as I know he never did.

Ed would regularly get colds when he was young, which meant Raymond and I would often go to mass on Saturday morning without him. On the way home my uncle would give us a nickel, or sometimes a dime, so we could buy donuts. Ray and I would each eat one and save the third for Ed—although I must confess, sometimes we thought he might be "too sick" to eat the donut, so we would eat it for him on the way home. May God forgive me.

My dad's mother was an Irish Catholic girl named Kate Fogerty. His father was a Lutheran from Bavaria who converted to Catholicism on his death bed. Before I began any kind of schooling, I knew how to make the sign of the cross, recite the Hail Mary, and say several childhood prayers. I never resisted any of this. It made me feel loved, by my parents and by God.

When I entered first grade, my parents naturally wanted to send me to Catholic school, but they didn't because my mother was pregnant with Raymond. I didn't know she was pregnant; parents didn't talk about those things with their children back then. It was a ten-block walk to school, and the road went through Market Street. There were no stoplights, and my parents were worried I might be run over, even though there weren't many cars around in those days. So instead I went to public school, which was only two blocks away. By second grade they must have thought I'd grown up enough to walk myself, so I started my Catholic education at Most Holy Redeemer School on Diamond Street.

Tuition was two dollars a month for me and one dollar per month for each of my brothers. My dad always insisted we pay in silver dollars because many of the nuns were from Chicago, and he didn't think they had ever seen silver dollars, which were minted in San Francisco. The school went from first through eighth grade. I loved school and wanted to do all my lessons well. I was an ordinary little girl who liked to have a good time, but if I didn't receive good grades, I felt disappointed. I worked very hard in school because I wanted to win a scholarship to Saint Paul's High School so my mom and dad wouldn't have to pay tuition. Eventually, I did win the scholarship and went to the all-girls school.

Growing up, I often enjoyed having company in the house; however, I didn't like that my mom had to work so hard to prepare food and be a good hostess. If I thought the guests were overstaying their visit, I would pipe up, "It's time for you to go home now." I was never one for holding my tongue.

We took regular walks with my dad through Buena Vista Park after dinner. One night my brothers and I asked him where we came from. He thought we were too young to hear the truth, so he said, "The doctor found you in a tree in Buena Vista Park. Then he took you to Saint Joseph's Hospital and gave you to Mom." After that, there were quite a few times when my brothers and I would run around the park looking in those trees trying to find the newborn babies. My dad would simply shake his head and say, "Looks like we got here a little too late."

———

Although we knew our parents were in charge, I wouldn't describe them as strict. They didn't enforce a lot of rules; however, some rules were harder to follow than others. There was a door to the living room that they kept locked in the days leading up to Christmas. My father said it was Santa's workshop. One year it was getting close to the big day and my mom had to do some last-minute shopping. She left us at home with my grandfather. I was playing outside, and my grandfather got worried because my brothers were so quiet, so he went inside to see what they were up to. My brothers, wily devils that they were, figured out that the same skeleton key that opened the bathroom door worked on the living room door as well. My brothers ran outside excitedly and told me they saw they were getting bicycles.

When Christmas came, my father sadly informed my brothers that Santa Claus had not brought them any presents. He didn't explain why. My brothers were so crushed that I started to cry too. But my dad kept up the ruse. "I don't understand why Santa didn't bring you what you asked for while you sat on his lap," he said.

Finally, my brothers fessed up. They admitted to using the key to go into the living room. My father told them how disappointed he was—he already knew about it, of course—and they all agreed this was why Santa took back the presents.

Our family came over for dinner that night. As we were eating, our front doorbell rang. My father got up to answer it. When he returned, he said, "You'll never guess who was at the door. Santa!" My brothers' little faces lit up. They ran into the living room, and, sure enough, their bicycles were there. Apparently, Santa heard their confession, believed they had done their penance, and forgave them.

When Ed became a teenager, he joined a group that called themselves the Sheiks. I guess that would be considered a gang today, but they didn't cause any trouble. They did think they were pretty suave, though.

When I was growing up, we didn't see our friends after school. We said goodbye and walked home. And we certainly didn't call our friends when we got home. Although we had a phone in our house, we shared the line with our neighbors. Sometimes we'd pick up the phone and hear other people talking. Later on, even when we had our own phone, we had to put a nickel in the slot if we wanted to use it. Then the Great Depression happened, and we couldn't afford that, so we had the phone removed.

Like a lot of people who lived through the Depression, our family learned to appreciate what we had and also what we had to give up. We didn't go out to dinner unless it was a very, very special occasion. We'd go to an Italian restaurant, and the whole meal would cost two and a half dollars.

During that time, my dad was fortunate to keep his job as a janitor at the San Francisco Civic Auditorium. That and city hall were the two largest buildings in the city. The auditorium held many wonderful events. There was ice skating, bicycle races, graduations, the firemen's ball, the policemen's ball, and more. Later the city constructed a veterans building and an opera house, and my dad was moved into a position as a civic administrator. He became a very important official in the city.

Every year when the city held a big luncheon for its workers, it was pointed out that we were the family with the most people on staff. Two of my aunts were public school teachers. One taught first grade for forty-five years; the other taught junior high. One of my uncles was in housekeeping at city hall; the other drove a truck for the sanitation department. We were San Franciscans through and through. It wasn't just a big city for us—it was our community.

Looking back, it was very impressive my dad was able to provide so well for his family considering his education didn't extend beyond his junior year of high school. Instead, he had to go to work. My mom only went to school through seventh grade. It always amazed me how much psychology my mom knew even though she had never learned it in school.

As I said before, from the very start, I was an eager student in school. I thought I had the answers to everything. Once, a priest came to our class to talk about the Ten Commandments. "Moses had two tablets," he said, "but there were seven commandments on one and three on the other. Does anyone know why?"

No one raised a hand. I couldn't let everyone sit in silence like that, could I? I shot my hand in the air. "Well, seven plus three is ten," I said. "So whatever the reason, God got it right." Although the actual answer is that the first three refer to God and the other seven refer to man, my answer sounded pretty good at the time—at least to me.

Everywhere I turned, I was encouraged to reinforce my belief in the goodness and grace of God—that He always gets it right. I realize it's not easy for people to maintain belief, especially after someone they love dies. For those who respond to those situations by turning away from faith, I would suggest that maybe they should give God a second date. As painful as it is to lose someone we love, it's our mission to trust that God has His reasons for calling them home. That call will come for all of us—we just don't know when. God is full of surprises. Most of them are pleasant, but many are not. Either way death is out of our control. The only thing we can do in those moments is hold as hard as we can to belief.

I was especially close with my paternal grandmother, Kate. She was an active churchgoer and would often take me to a German church in San Francisco called Saint Boniface. Not only did she go to services often, she also went to almost every funeral in her parish, whether she knew the person well or not. When I asked her why, she replied, "Because not everyone has family. If I go to the funeral, I know that I am there to pray and pay my respects."

There was an important lesson in there for me. Sometimes the most important part of love is showing up.

Two

The Blessings of Acceptance

It's important to help others be happy.

I GREW UP IN what is now known as the Castro District of San Francisco. It was a very Catholic city back then. To this day there are many churches that were originally built by Italian and Irish immigrants. People came to America to be Americans, but they also brought their cultures from home. It made for a wonderful neighborhood featuring a mélange of flavors from across the world.

Our neighborhood comprised more than just Catholics. In fact, there was a strict Mormon family that lived right across the street from us. I felt sorry for them because it seemed like they had to do a lot of difficult stuff. For instance, one Sunday a month the dad tithed to their church, which meant his family couldn't have break-fast that day because money was tight.

My parents were incredibly understanding and accepting

people. From the start, they emphasized to my brothers and me the idea that we should accept everyone no matter who they are, what they believe, who they love, and how they pray. We were not to look down on anyone for not being Catholic or for being "less Catholic" than we were. We didn't talk disparagingly about anybody who was different. If we had, I'm sure our parents wouldn't have stood for it. They emphasized that God made every one of us out of love. My mom told us, "We need to love God back, because He made you out of love. We have so much for which to be grateful." My dad would add, "People may believe in a different kind of God, maybe they look at Him in a different way, but it's still the same God." My dad looked at the earth and the trees and the water and knew that only God could make such beautiful things. There was no other possible explanation.

I don't recall my parents ever using the word *diversity*. We were taught to be so accepting of differences that we hardly noticed them. All the kids in the neighborhood played together, boys and girls. We enjoyed playing touch football. Usually the teams were coed, but sometimes we played boys against the girls. We girls always wanted to beat the boys, that's for sure. But I don't remember there ever being a single fight.

Most of the kids I knew went to public school. I was blessed to be raised in a community filled with immigrants from all over the world. This taught me the importance of acceptance. If you didn't accept the differences between your neighbors, you were going to have a hard time getting along. There were several French families in our neighborhood who sent their kids to French schools. There were also a lot of Chinese and Japanese people living in San Francisco. We loved going to Chinatown. We had Japanese twins in our first-grade class named Mizuki and Mazaki. When we took our class picture, the two of them stood at opposite sides, like bookends.

There were not many Black people living in our neighborhood at that time, however. Many of the Black people in the Bay Area lived in Oakland, where the fathers often worked as longshoremen. Their children went to school over there, but in time a few Black families moved closer to us. My aunt, who was a first-grade teacher, had a Black girl in her class named Helen. My aunt thought it was important for me and my brothers to spend time with people who were different, so she invited Helen over for dinner. I remember we had our picture taken together, and I thought Helen was a very sweet girl.

Sadly, I think our society has become more suspicious since then. People point to groups of other people and say they are the cause of so much trouble. Although that's not true, it's become the reaction to seeing people who come from a different culture. That's unfortunate. I wish we could be more accepting of one another.

My elementary school, Most Holy Redeemer, doesn't exist as a school anymore, but the church still stands. It now describes itself as an inclusive Catholic community and is considered one of the foremost parishes for LGBTQ people in the entire world. There were a lot of gay men living in our community when I was growing up, although I'm not sure I understood exactly what that meant at the time. I did know that some of the adults in town were concerned about them. We were told that if one of those men followed us to school or tried to talk to us, we should report them to our teachers or someone in authority.

Many of those fellas would talk to us after school, and I thought they were very nice. Finally one day I said to my dad, "You know, these guys are always talking to us, but they seem okay."

My dad replied, "If anybody tried to harm you, those men would be the first ones to help."

———

I don't pretend to know what God thinks about everything, but I do believe He created each one of us out of love. It's up to us to learn to accept people, no matter how different they are. Acceptance has to come from the heart. If we see someone who is different, we should try to remind ourselves that God created us just as unique as that person.

I see people express harsh feelings toward those from other cultures, and it breaks my heart. We forget that Jesus made friends with everybody. He would cure anybody who came along, even though it made the scribes and the Pharisees angry. This shows how accepting He was, and that should be our example.

My parents constantly reinforced this notion, not only with their words but, more importantly, through their actions. Neighbors were truly neighbors in our day. We knew everyone on our block. The parents all knew one another, and all the kids played together, even if we didn't go to the same school.

When I was ten, we moved into a house that had a garage. On Monday nights, my dad would host what he called his Blue Jamboree. He took his radio and attached it to a big megaphone so everyone could hear. He'd set up chairs for the neighbors, and they would all come and listen to the music. He wanted to create that sense of community. We thought our dad was the smartest guy on the block.

My mom was also a very happy person. She always found solutions to problems. That was especially important during the Great

Depression. My brothers and I would help my mom bring the groceries home from the store. We'd ask, "Do you think we can have an ice cream cone today?" Those cones cost a nickel, and oftentimes she didn't have one. So she'd answer, "I don't think we can today, but when we get home, I'll make some snickerdoodles. How does that sound?"

She tried not to say no to us unless she had to, but when she did that was okay. Boys and girls have to hear the word *no* sometimes. Still, she didn't like to say it. This meant sometimes she'd say instead, "Ask your father." When we'd ask Dad, he'd say, "I think you better ask your mother."

During the Depression, we knew we couldn't have everything we wanted. My mother would send us to the store with five cents. We would buy vegetables, which she would make into a big pot of soup that lasted for two days. Then she'd send us with another five cents to the butcher to buy meat bones. We skimped as best we could, but my dad was insistent that we would always pay our school tuition. We still attended mass regularly and gave what little we had to the church. Through it all, we learned the value of money.

During this time, despair was all around, and people were desperate to get by. I remember one of my aunts was robbed on her way home from work. You could look into the hills and see people sleeping there. We called them hobos. I was too young to really understand, so I don't think I was necessarily frightened, but I knew that something was not right. However, I also saw a lot of goodness in our community. People had block parties and shared their food and vegetables with their neighbors. We never visited anyone's house without bringing something. Even in the worst of times, people wanted to help one another. After our phone was disconnected, our next-door neighbor, Mrs. Kraeger, told my mom, "Whenever you want to use the telephone, just come on over. And you can give my number to your friends in case of emergency. If someone calls here for you, I'll let you know."

It was a good lesson for me at a young age. Times may be bad, but people are still good.

When I was about ten years old, I overheard a conversation at a picnic indicating that an older girl we knew named Ann-Marie was going to have a baby. I said to my mom, "How can Ann-Marie have a baby if she's not married?" My mom replied, "I don't want you to worry about Ann-Marie. She's going to have the baby, and she's going to be a very good mother."

Looking back, I think that was her way of telling me that Ann-Marie was not going to have an abortion. She was telling me in so many words that I shouldn't consider myself superior because of what Ann-Marie was experiencing. My mom always told us that if we saw people in trouble, we should care for them and try to help. And that if we were good to other people, they would be good to us.

I believe we should be tolerant of other people's mistakes. Saint Paul and Saint Peter made mistakes. Peter denied Jesus—that was a big one. Too often we think of God as a very stern judge. I think in many ways, though, we're getting back to the spirit of acceptance in the church. Still, sometimes people are so overpowering in their religion, it's a challenge for others to listen. But you can't be tough on everybody. It's like a mother who has many children. She can't treat them all the same, but she can love them all the same.

Many churches are having a harder time getting people to come for services, especially younger people. We have to do better. If we don't welcome and love our young people through their tough times, I'm worried we might lose a generation.

I get sad when somebody makes a mistake. I don't like to say they did something wrong—I call it a mistake. I pray that the person will find a path toward joy and happiness. But that doesn't mean I condemn or judge them. You have to live according to the way you believe. Believe in life, believe in God, believe in the future. In doing so, it's important to help others find happiness.

As I look back on those early years, I can see where I was given a foundation that continues to serve me to this day. My office at Loyola is in the student union and has a nice window and a door that is always open. From where I sit behind my desk, I can see the students come and go. They sit at the tables to congregate, eat, and study. They see me in my office and know they can come in and talk to me anytime. People wander in and out all day, the phone is constantly ringing, there's a steady buzz of activity all around. In many ways, that office is like my father's garage. I may not have a radio with a megaphone as he did, but I'm part of a lovely neighborhood.

San Francisco didn't feel like a big city when I was young. Developers were afraid that if they put up too many buildings, the buildings would be destroyed by earthquakes. If you wanted to go across the bay, you had to take a ferry. I loved riding the ferry. We'd drive our car onto the boat and ride across. We had a Star car in those days. It was built by the Durant Motor Company during the 1920s as a competitor to the Ford Model T. Before my mom married, she used a horse and a motorcycle to get around. Yes, a motorcycle.

That changed when they built the Golden Gate Bridge. We went out there often and watched them build it. The men would go out on those catwalks and work all the time, including weekends, because they were in a hurry to get it done. We would ride by the building site and marvel at how those men worked up so high using the suspension cables. I thought I'd get terribly dizzy if I tried that.

It was very exciting when they opened the bridge to the public on May 27, 1937. They let everyone walk across. I had to pay a nickel, but my mom paid a quarter. It was an exciting day, but I was sad I wouldn't be riding the ferry anymore. I had always looked forward to that.

Back then most moms didn't work, but when I was in seventh grade, my mom got a job as a clerk in the Weinstein Company Department Store on Market Street. During that time my brothers and I had to help a lot more with the housework and figure out how to help our dad. After a couple of weeks, Mom started getting bad headaches. My father suggested she leave the job because it was causing her too much stress. To make things easier on her, he had us do laundry on Sundays. I mentioned to him that as Catholics, we weren't supposed to work on the Sabbath. He smiled and said, "God will understand."

My family had an ark. No, there was no great flood or many pairs of animals on board, but it was a wonderful place for all the relatives to get together. My dad and his brother bought the ark for $625. It was docked on a main tributary of the San Francisco Bay. They felt like it was too expensive to travel and go on vacations all the time, so this became our vacation spot for the entire family.

The name of the ark was *Pastime*. There were sleeping ports and a nice living room, bedroom, and kitchen. There was a stove, a refrigerator, and a few other appliances on board. The hull was filled with mud to keep the ark from floating away. When the tide came in, we would all go swimming.

We made wonderful memories with that ark over many decades. There was a bridge nearby that led to hills that were owned by the Archdiocese of San Francisco. It was a great place to hike, but we had to go early in the morning before it got too hot. My grandfather and I would get up at 5 a.m. and go pick blackberries. We'd bring them back to the ark, and my mom would make a pie for dinner. I can still remember the smell of that kitchen when she cooked them.

We also had a motorboat. My dad used it take us out fishing on the bay. We would pass San Quentin prison. Some days you could see the inmates playing basketball during their recreation time. Once in a while the sirens from the prison would go off, which meant a prisoner had escaped. We'd be scared out of our wits and run back to the ark hoping the guy wouldn't show up.

During this time we had a pet monkey named Jerry. We got Jerry from a friend who was an engineer on a cargo boat that made trips to South America. Jerry was small but very active. He got nervous if there were too many people around, so we kept him in a cage in the basement. He was used to the heat, and he became uncomfortable when the weather in San Francisco turned cold. So my mom made him a red sweater to keep him warm. She also gave him a baby blanket, which she would wrap around him when he slept. We weren't sure what to feed him, but our friend from the boat said they had fed the monkey coffee and toast. That's what he had every morning. He especially liked it when my mom put sugar in his coffee. He'd dip his toast in the coffee and eat it, and then hold two hands on the cup and take a sip.

Jerry liked women more than men, and if he smelled liquor on anybody, he squealed like you wouldn't believe. I guess he was a teetotaler.

My dad built Jerry a cage outside so he could play in it. He had a little swing and a slide, and he jumped around all day. The kids in the neighborhood loved coming over to play with him, and my mom would bring him into school so the sisters and all the kids could see him. We had Jerry for about five years until one day somebody cut a hole in the top of the cage and stole him. We were heartbroken.

Our next pet was a puppy. He was adorable, but he cried all night long, so my dad gave him back. We never got another dog. We did, however, have a chicken pen outside our house. We had three chicks, three ducks, and three rabbits. Our aunts and uncles would occasionally come over with another animal for the pen. There was a deep well in the hills near us where we could go fishing. If we gave the man who owned the land a nickel, we could keep all the goldfish we caught.

We were very lucky our parents bought a house when I was two, not only so we could have a menagerie of pets but also because it helped us financially. We owned a two-story flat and rented out the first floor for twenty-five dollars a month. It helped us get through the Depression. It became my job to ask the tenants for the rent money. I guess that made me the "muscle" of the family.

I have been blessed in more ways than I could possibly count, but being born into such a large family is definitely near the top of the list. I was never bored, never lonely, and I never had any doubt what was expected of me. I was taught from the start that loving and caring for family was an important part of serving God. I'm grateful for the memories and especially for the values my relatives passed along. They wanted me to be accepting, loving, and kind to everyone I met. Many of those family members are gone now, but I'd like to believe that I'm still carrying on their legacy. Wherever I go, whatever I do, their love and teachings—and the ark—is always with me, still keeping me afloat.

Three

The Power of Dreams

A dream without a plan is just a dream.

I HEARD A PARABLE once about a young boy whose family owned horses. These were regular workhorses, but this boy dreamed of owning racehorses someday. So he wrote a paper about it for a classroom assignment. The teacher gave him an F and said, "Write something else. This dream will never come true."

The boy was extremely distraught. He went home and asked his father what he should do. His father told him, "You have to decide for yourself." The boy thought about it for a few days and then handed in the same paper. He wrote a note at the top saying, "You can give me an F." Then he went out and fulfilled his dream.

My life is a testament to the power of dreams. Mine came to me when I was in the third grade. We had a teacher in school named

Sister Mary Patrize. She was a member of the Sisters of Charity of the Blessed Virgin Mary. Everyone loved her. She was young and beautiful and so much fun. When we found out at the beginning of the year that she was going to move with us into fourth grade, we all cheered. We had been worried we were going to get a crabby sister.

Sister Mary Patrize used to tell us that even though we were in third grade, we were not too young to be thinking about what we wanted to be when we grew up. "How many of you are going to be policemen?" she asked. A few hands went up. She continued: "How many of you are going to be firemen? How many of you are going to be priests? How many of you are going to be sisters? How many of you are going to be doctors? How many of you are going to be nurses?" It was her way of getting us to think along these lines, although no girls at that time would raise their hand to be a doctor. (I'm very glad that has changed!)

I was so fond of Sister Mary Patrize that my decision was easy: I wanted to become a BVM sister, just like her. I had some familiarity with the religious life because several people in my family had chosen that path. My mom had a sister who was a Notre Dame sister on the East Coast. She had a niece who was also a Notre Dame sister. My dad had a sibling who was a Holy Family sister. So this was not something out of the ordinary for me. I had an aunt on my dad's side who was a catechism teacher. I knew I didn't want to do that, but I knew I wanted to teach, preferably English and math. I was forever playing school with my brothers and the other kids in the neighborhood. I was always the teacher, and they had to obey me.

Sister Mary Patrize said we should pray to God every day and ask Him to guide us. So I would pray, "Dear God, help me understand what I should do, but please tell me that I should become a BVM sister." I guess God listened to me on that one.

There weren't many career options for young women at that time. We could become nurses, teachers, secretaries, or moms— that was about the extent of it. I knew if I became a sister, it meant not getting married or becoming a mother, but I had no desire for those things. I was prepared for a lifetime commitment. Anything less than total devotion would not have worked.

I had my first experience as a teacher when I was twelve years old. One of the sisters in our school needed to accompany a retired sister to attend to her dying mother, and I was asked to take over her first-grade class. All I had to do was follow the instructions the teacher left for me. What experience did I have? Well, I played school with my brothers and other kids on the block. That was it. But I found that I had a knack for directing people, not as a stern authoritarian but in a loving, caring way. A skill I learned from my parents.

When I was a junior in high school, I thought it would be a neat surprise gift for our teacher if the class presented a program for her. On the big day, I asked her if I could take over the class, and she agreed without asking why. All the students cooperated, and she was pleased I ran the program.

The next year, I was placed in charge of the school bookstore. I clerked there each morning. When one of our sisters was injured and we became shorthanded, the principal asked me to supervise a daily freshman study hall. I was pretty good at Latin, and they figured I could help the freshmen when they had a question on that subject.

Each time I had one of these experiences, it reinforced that my dream was the right dream for me. All I had to do was put together my plan and work hard to follow it, and I would be on my way.

My parents also fostered in me a love of sports. They were great football fans. We listened to games on the radio all the time. They also took us to games at Kezar Stadium. One time Saint Mary's College needed money for their football team, so they asked the Archdiocese of San Francisco if Catholic school children could go to their game against Washington as a way to raise money. Our entire school took the day off and rode streetcars to the stadium, and we all paid a dime so we could go inside and watch. I sat next to my teacher and explained to her everything that was happening, since I knew the rules and she didn't. Our field trip gave Saint Mary's enough money to keep the program going.

In our world, there was nothing bigger than Notre Dame football. When the Fighting Irish were playing, the world stopped. As a little girl I assumed Notre Dame won every single game, based on the way the sisters talked about the team. On Saturday, they would say the Rosary and pray for the Fighting Irish to win. Then they'd come in on Monday and report that they did—again.

I used to ask the sisters, "Did you pray for Notre Dame to win?" They always said yes—and Notre Dame almost always won. Maybe that was a coincidence, but I didn't think so.

I will never forget the day when I heard the news that Knute Rockne, the legendary Notre Dame football coach, had died in a plane crash. It was Tuesday, March 31, 1931. I had gone to my grandma's house for lunch and heard the news on the radio. I raced back to school and said to the other children, "Knute Rockne died. We have to let the sisters know." I was told they were having lunch. We never disturbed the sisters while they were eating, but I thought this was important. So I took a deep breath, knocked on the door, and delivered the sad news.

I never thought about whether it was normal or common for a young girl to be so interested in sports—and as far as I could tell, no one else did, either. I loved the games and the social experience, but I also fell in love with competition. I liked that the scoreboard showed in the clearest of terms who won and who lost. I believed winning wasn't everything and losing wasn't the end of the world, because there was always another game to play.

My ninth-grade class consisted of 135 girls. We were the largest incoming class the school had ever welcomed, which we thought was pretty impressive. The sisters in the school taught us every subject except for gym. However, there was a woman who came in once a week to teach us physical education because the sisters wanted to be sure we got some exercise.

Things seemed pretty simple at school. There were no boys, and I wasn't interested in boys anyway because I knew I wanted to be a BVM sister. We went to parties sometimes, but everybody was invited. There were no cliques. All of our parents knew one another, so we would know if someone was having a party. Our parties were very harmless. You didn't see a lot of alcohol back then, and I never heard about anyone doing drugs.

Saint Paul's had a varsity basketball team, but I had never played before so I didn't bother trying out. I did, however, sign up for the intramural team. The sport of basketball was still quite young—James Naismith had invented it in Springfield, Massachusetts, in

1891—and the girls' version was much different from the boys' version. For girls' basketball, the court was divided into three zones, and each player could only play in one of them. There were two forwards and two guards at each end, and then two centers in the middle along with two others whose position was called "sides." Although they made those rules for girls because they didn't think that we were as strong physically as the boys, girls and women have since proven that they can do a lot of things that people didn't think they were able to do.

When playing basketball, I was a side. When I got the ball I would pass it to the center, who had to pass the ball to a forward because only forwards were allowed to make shots. If I stepped over the line, then my team lost the ball. So it was far more of a passing game than a dribbling game. I think that's why I've always preferred to watch basketball teams that are skilled at passing.

Most of all, I like that most sports require teamwork. That's what life is all about. Families have to have teamwork. Husbands and wives have to have teamwork. Businesses have to have teamwork. Sports encourage all of that. We say all the time at Loyola, "No one person can do it alone. It has to be the whole group together." You have to take things one game at a time. And if you lose, you have to be a good sport about it. You can't mope around afterward. You have to pick up the pieces and get going again.

There are so many benefits to competition. It really helps develop life skills. If we sit back and don't compete, our character doesn't grow. That's why I believe competition should start when children are young.

Losing is tough no matter how or when it happens. If you play a game, there is going to be a winner and a loser. But so long as that's the case, I'd much rather win.

By the time I was a senior in high school, I was ready to convert my dream into a plan. Being a BVM sister required enrolling at the Mount Carmel Motherhouse in Dubuque, Iowa. I didn't know anything about Iowa—I just knew that's where my teachers had studied, and therefore I wanted to study there as well.

When I informed one of the sisters of my plan, she asked, "Did you write and ask if you could come?" I was confused. What did she mean, "write and ask"? I thought I could just show up.

She shook her head. "No, you need permission," she said. "Write them a letter." I did as she said, and a few weeks later I received an acceptance letter in the mail.

The BVM community was founded by five Irish women who opened a school in Dublin, Ireland, in 1831. Two years later, they met a Catholic priest from Philadelphia. He told them about the struggles of Irish Catholic immigrants in America and invited them to cross the Atlantic and plant their gospel. We were always told the story of Eliza Kelly, who was entrusted with the purse that held all their money. When the ladies arrived in Philadelphia harbor, Eliza walked down the rope ladder to take them to the boat that would carry them ashore, and she accidentally dropped the purse with all their money into the ocean. Imagine her despair!

The sisters taught the children of other Irish immigrants in Philadelphia. Several years later they moved to Iowa and established

their community. As more and more women entered the congrega-
tion, the original building couldn't contain them all, so they built a
bigger place at Mount Carmel, and it grew from there.

Two other girls from my high school, Nora Sheehan and Dolores
Black, also enrolled at Mount Carmel. We had to take a ferry boat
from San Francisco to Oakland and then a train from Oakland to
Grand Island, Nebraska. From there, we transferred to another train
that transported us to Dubuque.

The area was gorgeous. The building was nice and the grounds
were very well-kept. It sat on charming bluffs overlooking the
Mississippi River. There was even an apple orchard on the property.
Our own little garden of Eden!

Our entrance day was September 8, 1937. There were forty-five
of us who entered the motherhouse that day. Most of us had just
finished high school, although a few had gone to college. We had to
bring with us all the things we needed, including blankets, pillows,
and towels. Our moms also had to make our postulant habits. My
mom learned to make mine with the help of a neighbor who had
three daughters who became sisters. She packed it into my trunk
with the rest of my belongings and shipped it to Dubuque.

Four days after we entered, we were given our habits. Eight to
ten of us were assigned to each dormitory. For the next six months
we served as postulants, beginning our education on what religious
life was all about. Our Postulant Directress taught us the process of
meditating. She wanted us to meditate for a half hour each morning,
which at the time seemed like an eternity.

The facility in Dubuque has been described as a convent, but
that is not true. It's a motherhouse, created to educate future sisters. I've been called a nun so often that I use the word to describe

myself, but it's also inaccurate. Technically, I'm a sister, not a nun. The difference is that a nun lives more of a contemplative life in prayer and solitude. That would never have worked for me. I loved being around people too much, and I knew from the very beginning that I wanted to teach young kids. The BVM sisters were dedicated to doing just that.

Our days as postulants were very busy! They started with our wake-up call at 5 a.m. We were in the chapel by 5:20. Following prayers, meditation, and mass, we went to breakfast, which was served by the novices, who went table to table. After the meal, we all went out for a walk. That usually meant going down to the cemetery and praying for the deceased sisters. Then we put on what we called our "blues," which were blue aprons, and did our chores, which took a couple of hours and usually meant cleaning around the dormitory or classrooms. Then we came back for instructions before lunch. That meal, like all the meals, was conducted in silence.

From there, we attended afternoon classes. Classes were always in between chores and activities. We'd have one or two in the morning and then several after lunch. The sisters from Clarke College came over and taught us. They would tease us that we should all get good grades because we didn't go out like "normal" college students, but we let them know that we were kept plenty busy on that campus. We didn't have a ton of free time!

When evening came, we had private prayer time in the chapel, followed by dinner and spiritual readings. After an hour or so of recreation, we had spiritual reading time and then our nightly prayers. At 9 p.m. it was time for bed. We rarely had trouble falling asleep.

I didn't mind the work and the long hours, but I found myself wishing we had more time for studying. Besides our formation classes and other religious classes, we were taught English, history, and literature. Another priest from Loras College taught us philosophy of education and American education in order to get us ready to fulfill our mission of teaching.

We were also taught to be loving and to care for one another, and I honestly don't remember any bickering, maybe because there was really nothing to argue about. I made lots of friends among my fellow novices, and we kept in touch for a long time afterward, although I'm sad to say I'm the only one still living out of my group.

On weekend afternoons we would go for walks over the hills. Sometimes we'd walk as far as Julien Dubuque's grave, which was a couple of miles each way. It was lovely to be outside together on a sunny day with a soft breeze tickling the hills. We had various gardening projects where we turned some of the local land into gardens and responsible to keep them in proper shape. There wasn't much water supply, so we'd have to fill up buckets and carry them. In the winter when it snowed, we'd get sleds and ride down the hills together.

We also had to abide by a rule against talking. That was the hardest part for me. (No kidding, right?) The motherhouse is still operational, and I heard they got rid of the no talking rule. Good riddance, I say. Fortunately, we had a very generous Postulant Directress who had taught in a high school. She was in residence with the girls, so she knew a lot about young people. When she saw we were getting antsy, she would put a sign on the board that read "High Party." That meant we were to go up to the attic, have some treats, and socialize to our hearts' content. We were supposed to keep this a secret from the older sisters, but I'm sure they found out about it. Because of these special treats and hearty meals, we all gained some weight. In college today they call it the "Freshman Fifteen" because new students tend to gain fifteen pounds that first year. It was the same for the motherhouse.

Because the curriculum was so challenging, it forced us to decide whether this religious life was for us. For some of the girls there, it was too much, and a few of them decided to leave. That thought never once occurred to me. I really believed this was my proper vocation. I wanted to serve God and serve God's people.

I was there for two and a half years, and throughout that period I felt myself moving closer to God. What does that feel like? Well, for me, it's a feeling of relaxation, and most of all, just knowing I was on the proper course. It helped that no one, least of all my family, ever forced me into this choice. I never felt pressured to do it. It came 100 percent from within. I owned it, and I never questioned it. I knew I was in the right place and that the sacrifices I was making would set me up for a happy, purposeful life.

I wouldn't say I was homesick, but I definitely missed my family. My brother sent me *Henry* cartoons from the newspaper because he knew I loved them so much. I was pleasantly surprised when my mom came to see me one December. That was not the normal visiting time, but she had written to the Postulant Directress and said she missed her only daughter very much. She wanted to come and give me a Christmas present on her way to visiting her family in Philadelphia.

I was so delighted to see her. I met her in the Postulant Directress's office, where my mom gave the Directress a Christmas present. It was a box of walnuts, cookies, and an assortment of goodies. A short while later the Directress, Sister Angelice, came back holding up a bottle of whiskey she had found in the box. "What did you expect me to do with this?" she asked.

My mom was so embarrassed! She had given the Directress the wrong box, one she intended to give her sister in Philadelphia. She suggested to Sister Angelice that she could keep the bottle because the whiskey would help settle stomachs if someone got sick. The sister took her up on the idea.

My mom was there for the selection of my religious name. The Mother General asked her, "What kind of name would you like for your daughter?" My mom said she didn't want me to have her name. "That's okay," the Mother General said. "We already have a Sister Bertha."

My mom mentioned that I had always liked the name Dolores, but that wasn't an option because there were already a lot of combinations of that name. Finally, the Postulant Directress took her finger and ran it down a list of Christian names. She stopped it between Jane and Jean. She decided Jean sounded better. Sometimes I think about that moment and wonder how the Mother General would have reacted if she knew that some eighty years later millions of people would come to know the name "Sister Jean" just because a basketball team won a few games nobody thought it could win. I'm sure she would have gotten a kick out of it.

I was unable to visit my family during my stay at the motherhouse, but unlike many of the students who lived locally and were able to receive visits from their parents, I was allowed to talk on the phone to my parents several times. By that time my dad had become a deputy sheriff in San Francisco, and part of his job was to take prisoners back to their home cities after they got releases or for court dates. He took a few of them to Chicago, and when he did, he drove to Dubuque to see me.

I learned so much during my two and a half years at the motherhouse. For starters, I learned to get along with all kinds of people whose ideas were different from mine. I also learned the fundamentals of what it would take to become a good teacher. I knew this was the central part of my mission, and though I was looking forward to that, I had my doubts as to just how ready I was.

Most of all, my time in Dubuque taught me to love God even more. My relationship with God was evolving into a more mature one, less childlike. There's something to be said for a child's unabashed faith, but as we mature we understand what it really means to love God, just like we come to understand what it really means to love another person. I felt more invested in my relationship with God, and as a result I believed I could depend on Him more. It's kind of like a courtship. At first it's very intense, but as the relationship grows, it becomes deeper, more solid. It's not puppy love anymore.

In March 1940, I made my vows and was declared a Sister of Charity of the Blessed Virgin Mary—just like I had dreamed about in third grade. When I look back at this time in my life, I honestly can't believe that the dream that first came to me as a young girl put me on such a gratifying, godly path. All I ever wanted to do was serve God and teach children. I had my dream, but I also made my plans and worked very hard to see them through. This is what I try to teach the young people I talk to every day at Loyola. When one of them tells me about his or her dreams, I eagerly chime in, "Go for it! Go for your dreams! You'll always regret it if you don't." But I am quick to add that a dream without a plan is just a dream. Plans require action, and action requires persistence.

If you're lucky enough to have a dream that is so powerful you're willing to work for it, you end up with a life that is teeming with purpose. I thank God every day that He planted such a beautiful dream in my heart all those years ago and then blessed me with the fortitude to make it come true.

Four

Becoming a Teacher

Sometimes you need to speak quietly to be heard.

MY FIRST ASSIGNMENT AS a BVM sister was at Saint Vincent's school in Chicago teaching fifth grade. I was so nervous my first day, I overprepared for my reading lesson. I was worried I wouldn't have enough time. At the end of the day a little girl, Evelyn, came up to me and said, "Sister Jean, it's time to do the brushes." The first one in each row was given a handheld brush so that each student could sweep under their desks. The school didn't have a janitor, so they relied on the students to clean up at the end of the day. I was grateful for that little girl's help on my first day because I had a lot to learn about the daily routine.

I would never have made it through those first few months without Sister Laurena. She taught the other fifth-grade class and helped me with my lesson plans. Every Sunday we mapped out the week on

3x5 index cards. We gave the same exams on Fridays for math and English. Some of the teachers at Saint Vincent's were much older, and because of that, it seemed to me the children were running footloose and fancy-free. I felt that I needed to set a firmer tone. When I walked into the room, I made sure to get everybody settled. Then I could loosen things up as the school year went along.

I figured out early on that the key to being a good teacher was to make learning fun, especially when dealing with elementary school kids. There's only so much they can do if they feel like they have to grind their way through the day. This is a common mistake that teachers make—it's my way or the highway! I believe it's more effective to meet the students halfway. Actually, most of the time you have to meet them *all* the way. But that was okay with me. If you make them understand that you want them not only to learn but to *enjoy* learning, then they will do what you want. Well, mostly, anyway.

I remember one boy named Patrick who was especially rowdy. He was the youngest of seven children, so he was used to having to stand up for himself all the time. I asked the principal if she had any advice. She suggested I take a holy picture of Saint John Bosco and slip it into one of his schoolbooks. I'm not sure what that was supposed to accomplish, but when Patrick found it, he tore it up. However, I stayed with it, and I eventually wore him down. One day we were working through a challenging lesson on fractions. I was trying to explain the concept of inversions, but the students were confused. So I asked Patrick to come to the front of the room. Then I lifted him up and turned him upside down. "Here," I said. "This is what it means to invert fractions." I think the students understood it a little better after that.

I stayed in a very old house that used to be part of the school. There were twenty-one sisters living there, and the older ones had private rooms. Since I was new, I had a roommate, Sister Mary of the Angels. I knew her because she was a year ahead of me at the motherhouse, and we got along quite well.

The school was big, but it didn't have a playground. The streets had to be blocked off for recess so the children could play. The teachers were assigned what we called yard duty to make sure there weren't any fights. There was another sister there two years ahead of me named Sister Margaret. She and I used to play marbles together at recess with the boys. We had our own marbles, and the kids would gather around us to watch.

We weren't the only school in the area, so it was quite an active scene with all those rambunctious kids in the streets. Sometimes we let the kids from different schools play together. There would be a fight from time to time, but nothing too serious. I'd get in there and pull the kids apart, but I never got knocked over. I had brothers—I could more than hold my own.

Our students' families were mostly Irish. These immigrant families wanted to maintain a semblance of community. They raised enough money to build their own churches, which is why there are so many Catholic churches in Chicago today. I wasn't aware of any discrimination they faced, but I later learned it was happening.

The school was located in a poor neighborhood. A number of homeless men came to the house where we lived on Kenmore Avenue for lunch. We had a sister who cooked, and oftentimes she took care of the men. School tuition was around a dollar a month, and many of our families couldn't afford even that. Sometimes the parents would show up with a quarter because that was all they had, and we accepted it. Many of them came from big families, and in those days the moms didn't work, so it was up to the dads to feed all those hungry children.

We were blessed with a terrific principal and superior, Sister Mary Idus. She helped me learn that every little mishap was not a big tragedy. I was so young and eager, and I wanted everything to be perfect. I was not comfortable with my own limitations. Sister Mary Idus was a godsend. For example, she came to the rescue when it was time to put on a show for the school. The show didn't raise a lot of money, but people brought supplies that lasted us throughout the school year.

That year the play had a Native American theme, and I was charged with providing all the costumes. We got the materials, and one of the songs in that play was "God Bless America." I had never heard it before. Kate Smith had just recorded it, so I had to learn it along with the children. Even though we had what we needed, I was completely overwhelmed. Sister Mary Idus kept me calm and made sure I had all the resources I needed. Then when the night of the show came, I lost my voice, so Sister Mary Idus stepped in and made sure all the students knew where they were supposed to be. The show went beautifully.

As I was teaching, I continued my own education at DePaul University. I attended class each Saturday, learning a variety of subjects. As usual, I enjoyed math the most. I took an algebra class taught by a German man. He had a thick accent, so he was difficult to understand at times. One time he completed a problem on the board, and I asked him, "Why didn't you use the square root to get your answer?" He frowned and said, "What do you know about the square root?" I told him I had learned it in the eighth grade. He was so shocked, but he asked if anyone else knew what a square root was. None of them did. Score another one for California Catholic school education!

———

That first summer I was asked by the archdiocese to demonstrate religious lessons for the sisters who were going to teach middle grades in Chicago. I had taken a course during the first summer session, and the teacher suggested to my superior that I demonstrate the material to the older sisters during the Archdiocese Institute. There I was, a fresh-faced rookie standing in front of a room full of older sisters, teaching *them* how to teach. How intimidating! But they were incredibly accepting, and it did wonders for my confidence.

Every Saturday, all the sisters were invited to watch a movie at the Saint Ignatius Auditorium. We were not allowed to go to restaurants in those days; however, it was not something that bothered me or even surprised me. We knew this was the way our lives were going to be. We had made the choice to live this way.

All in all, I thought my first year as a sister and teacher was successful. I was looking forward to improving in year two, but before the year began, I received word that I was being sent to work at Saint Bernard School in Los Angeles. I had known at some point I would get assigned somewhere else, but I didn't know it would happen so quickly or be so far away. That was a very early introduction into life as a BVM sister. Wherever the BVMs wanted me to live and work, and whenever they wanted me to be there, that's where I would be.

I wasn't at Saint Vincent's long, but I learned a lot. The biggest thing I learned was to be patient with myself. There was so much I didn't know and had to improve upon, but I had to trust that God would get me there eventually.

I had only visited Southern California twice as a child, but I knew that living there would make it easier for my parents to visit me, so that made me happy. Saint Bernard's was so brand-new it was barely a school. The only part of the building that existed when I got there in the fall of 1941 was the foundation. The first and second grade teachers from Chicago taught in a feed and fuel store. The third through sixth grade teachers worked in a parish hall without any partitions to separate the classes. The principal taught seventh and eighth grade in the dining room of a small bungalow. It was not the most comfortable situation.

There were four of us who opened the new school—the principal, Sister Mary Gilbert, who came from Milwaukee; a third and fourth grade teacher from Kansas City; and two of us from Chicago. We were thrown together and started building our community. Since there were no living quarters, we lived in a convent in Pasadena, which was quite a distance, especially with the freeways always so crowded. We weren't allowed to drive, so we had to depend on mothers of students to help us make the long commute.

Besides our cramped, overcrowded physical space, we were dealing with students who were behind in their studies. The city of Los Angeles had an inadequate public school system, so when the children transferred in, they weren't prepared for the kind of work we required of them. We were supposed to give them end-of-year exams, but the archdiocese excused us as a school that first year. They also excused us from teaching geography because they wanted us to spend more time on English and math. That helped us and the students tremendously.

Once again, I was blessed to work for a kind, patient principal who served as an excellent mentor. She knew I was young, and she guided me while also letting me find my own way. She was experienced with establishing discipline, which was critical given our circumstances. She made announcements in the yard and spoke in a low, measured voice. You'd think she would need to shout, but she never raised her voice. That made the children listen more intently. I learned from her that sometimes you need to speak quietly to be heard.

With the many kids and a little space, I had to learn quickly about keeping youngsters in line. My parents' sensitive touch was effective, but it also had its limits. I recall a particular student who was constantly getting out of hand. He was a good boy, but he was, shall we say, rather spirited. I tried everything I could think of, but nothing worked. So I decided to pin him to my apron. For a whole week, he was not allowed to leave my side. That straightened him out for sure.

When the sisters wanted to relax and entertain ourselves, we would often see a movie provided by the local studios. Bing Crosby was a particular favorite. We also brought in movies from various studios, usually by parents of our students who worked in show business. The archbishop set up these showings; however, he didn't want us walking around Hollywood Boulevard. I guess he thought that was too sinful. We had a movie projector at the convent, and we watched films there, or sometimes we brought the projector to the school. It was a simple life with simple pleasures, just as I imagined it would be.

———

Everything changed for us, and the world, on December 7, 1941. We were assembled at Incarnation Church in Glendale, celebrating the Feast of the Immaculate Conception, when we heard the news about the bombing of Pearl Harbor. Being in California, we were worried that bombs could be dropped on us as well. We got all the children to their homes as quickly as we could, and then we hunkered down in anticipation of what would come next.

There were so many ways the war impacted us. For starters, all of our students had to wear dog tags that had their names and telephone numbers engraved on them. They did this in case we were bombed. Those were not easy conversations. The students were told to walk to and from school on the same road every day. That way if something happened, we knew where to find them. Some children were afraid to go to school alone, so they would travel in groups. We understood the children might be frightened, but we had to do our best to prepare for the worst. I tried to soothe their fears by saying, "Your mom will take care of you, we will take care of you, and God will take care of you."

Many of the dads were sent off to fight the war. That meant many of the moms had to enter the workforce. This is when the term *latchkey kid* was coined. It was used to describe children who wore keys around their necks so they could get into their homes when the parents were away. We kept blankets and food at the school in case we had to spend the night there in an emergency, but thankfully we never had to.

Everyone did their part to chip in. There was a lot of rationing, and we were given stamps to use at the store and trade in for groceries and other goods. We bartered with each other using those stamps. I owed our butcher so many tickets, it's a wonder I didn't go to jail.

Every Thursday morning the city siren went off at ten thirty for a bomb drill. When that happened, the children hunkered below their desks and stayed there until we heard the "all clear" signal. If a blackout was in place, everything would go dark late in the afternoon and remain that way until the following morning.

During the blackouts, there were no curfews, but we were not allowed to turn on our lights at night. Blackout watchers walked the streets, and if you had any light coming from your house, even a pilot flame on a boiler, they asked you to turn it off. When we had morning mass during a blackout, we sat there in the dark as the priest held up a candle and read from his book.

I remember hearing that the government was rounding up our Japanese neighbors and putting them into internment camps. We all thought that was wrong, and looking back on it today, it seems especially awful. Those people hadn't done anything wrong. It shows how the fear of the unknown can cause people to make awful decisions.

We dealt with our students' fears the only way we could, and that was by engaging in open conversation. We didn't hide or sugarcoat what was going on. We explained the situation to them clearly and told them it was okay to be afraid. We encouraged them to share their feelings.

The grown-ups were pretty rattled too. Although that period in our lives was a challenge, I don't remember hearing a lot of complaining. Back then people understood we had a collective responsibility to take care of one another. There weren't all these arguments about wanting to do things of your own free will or not wanting to be told by the government what to do. There was a war going on, and we were all in it together.

Both my brothers served in the navy during the war. My younger brother was only seventeen when he enlisted. Enlistees were supposed to be at least eighteen, but the military needed young soldiers so badly that nobody checked. Raymond was serving on a ship just off the coast of Japan when the US dropped a nuclear bomb on Hiroshima. He actually saw the mushroom cloud. He and Ed rarely talked about their war experiences, and we knew not to ask about them. They had seen such horrendous things, and I understood why they wouldn't want to relive it.

Naturally, my parents and I were worried for my brothers' safety while they were away. My parents never knew where Raymond was, but Ed was able to clue them in to his location thanks to a little secret code they had worked out before he left. Ed would write them letters that included several girls' names. The first letter of those names spelled out where Ed was stationed. I prayed every day my brothers would return home safe and sound. We were very lucky they made it through the war. Many others were not so fortunate. When the war was over, a chaplain who had served on my brother's ship came through California and visited all the families of the sailors who had lost their lives.

I was attending a retreat in Dubuque during the summer of 1945, preparing to make my perpetual vows with my fellow BVM sisters, when we were suddenly greeted by the sound of multiple sirens blasting from all over. It signified the end of the war. We made our way back to the motherhouse feeling exhilarated.

However, I had mixed emotions on hearing the news. On the one hand, of course I was thrilled that the war was finally over, not least because it meant my brothers would be returning home. But I also shuddered to think about what mankind had created. The atomic bomb was something we had never seen before. It meant that human civilization now had the means to destroy itself. I prayed for all the Japanese people who were killed by those two explosions. War is such an awful, awful thing. I pray often that there will come a day when there will be no more wars, but I don't think I'll live long enough to see it.

For a long time after the war, it was hard for Raymond to stop thinking of Japan as the enemy. As America's relationship with Japan started to mend, Raymond insisted he would never go over there. Many years later, his son Rich graduated from San Diego State University and decided to go to Japan to teach English. It was supposed to be a temporary assignment, but Rich liked it so much that he stayed. He established a very successful import/export business, and he met a lovely Japanese girl. She was a Buddhist, and in her culture it was tradition for the groom's father to ask the bride's father permission for the couple to marry. So Raymond flew to Japan, made the traditional request, and attended their wedding. He was supportive of the marriage and came away impressed by how Japan had rebuilt their country. The experience totally changed his feelings about Japan.

This is why we say love conquers all!

Five

Coach Jean

Fear is a lousy motivator.

PARENTS WERE UNDERSTANDABLY RELUCTANT to transfer their children to a brand-new private Catholic school, but once we established our reputation at Saint Bernard's, our student population grew quickly. The school building was finished that first year, and then we continued to add more space each year that followed. So many families signed up that we had to set up extra classrooms in the parish hall, where I taught fifth and sixth grades. It was quite a task to teach a double grade. I really had to be on my toes at all times.

I had a great experience at Saint Bernard's, but in the fall of 1946, I was transferred to Saint Charles Borromeo School in North Hollywood. I was assigned to teach eighth grade. At first I resisted, pointing out to my principal that I had never taught eighth grade before. "That's okay," she said. "I'll be here to help." I was going to teach the same subjects I taught in fifth grade, only at more advanced levels. I studied hard to prepare for that school year because I wanted to make sure those boys and girls would be successful when they moved on to high school.

Once again, the school was quite new, and because building production was limited during the war, the sisters taught in Quonset huts. Saint Charles was in an upscale neighborhood and, this being Hollywood, we had lots of children whose parents were celebrities. Bob Hope had two students there, one boy and one girl, as well as two younger children in the lower grades. The Hopes had a nice baseball field on their property where our boys played their games, since our schoolyard was just a few blocks away. We had a father-daughter dance that first year, and Bob came with his daughter Linda. His wife, Dolores, told me beforehand that he would be too shy to go, but she was only kidding.

Bob Hope was a great guy. He was always trying to be a good father. If he was in town, he and his wife almost always sat for dinner with the family. Bob was not a Catholic at the time, but his wife was, and their son, Tony, learned to be an altar boy. Bob came to every mass that Tony was assigned to. He was very proud of his son.

We all knew he was a big celebrity, of course. He seemed normal to me, but some people were starstruck when he was around. One day a fifth-grade boy ran up to his car and asked for an autograph. "Sure," Bob said. "What would you like me to sign?" The only thing the boy had was a geography book, so that's what Bob signed. At the end of the school year, when it was time for the students to give back their textbooks, this boy told his teacher, "I'm sorry, I can't give this book back to you."

"Why?" the teacher replied. "Is it because you like geography so much?"

"No, it's because Mr. Hope signed it," the boy said. So the sister tore out the page where Bob had signed, handed it to the boy, and collected the textbook.

The Sinatra kids and the Crosby kids were all in our local schools as well. I also taught the future cardinal Roger Mahony, who went on to become archbishop of Los Angeles.

While the new school was being built, we held class in a house across the street from the church. There wasn't enough room for all the desks, requiring us to set up benches, with six students per bench. The rows were so tight, if someone was sitting in the middle of the bench and had to go to the restroom, all the kids would have to stand up to let him or her pass.

It was a chaotic situation, to say the least, but by then I was accustomed to chaos. It was important that I made sure the students knew who was the boss—in my gentle way, of course. For example, when I walked in the first day, they were chattering away. I looked at the class and said, "I think I'm going to go out and come back in again so there won't be any talking." I did so, and it was quieter, but there was still some chatter. "Hmm, why don't I try that again," I said. I walked out and walked back in, this time to proper silence.

As far as I was concerned, the kids could have all the fun they wanted outside the classroom, but in my class I wanted them to be focused and studious. I noted that many of the boys were wearing blue jeans. "There will be no more blue jeans in this room," I declared. "Tomorrow I want you all to come in here wearing corduroy pants or slacks." To be honest, I had just assumed that there was a rule at the school against wearing blue jeans, since that was the case at my previous jobs.

Later that afternoon while having lunch at the convent, the principal approached me with the pastor alongside. "What did you tell the children today?" he asked. I reported that I had explained to the students what we would be learning during the school year, and that it took me three times to enter the room so they would be quiet.

"Did you tell them they couldn't wear blue jeans?" he asked.

"Oh, that. Yes, I did," I replied.

"Well, I had calls from several mothers saying, 'Who is this young nun telling my children what to do?'" he said. "I wanted to find out what happened before I answered them."

He wasn't angry with me. In fact, he assured me that he would back me up on this. "If you can get them to do this, that would be a real plus," he said. I stood my ground, and the students did as I asked.

Our principal, Sister Florence, required us to submit lesson plans for the week each Sunday. She examined the plans and returned them to us on Monday mornings with comments and suggestions. The guidance was extremely helpful. We were a group of young sisters who were figuring things out as we went along. Even though we were teachers, we were students as well, which is just how we liked it.

Our principal was innovative. We were doing departmental teaching long before many other schools started doing it. For example, I was assigned to teach math in grades five through eight. Every day I cycled through those rooms, and someone else came into my room to teach other subjects like English or civics. I taught reading and manuscript writing to the first-grade room, and the first-grade teacher went to my room to teach singing.

This was far different from the way most schools operated, which was to have the same teacher in the class all day rotating through all the subjects. Our principal was fearful that if we stuck with that model, the teachers would get bored with what they were doing, and the students would get tired of hearing the same voice in the front of the room. Her method kept things fresh for everyone.

The students responded well to the adjustment. One day I asked a first-grade boy how he liked the change. When he said he liked it very much, I asked him why. "Because," he answered, "if a sister gets mad at me in the morning, she doesn't see me until the end of the day, and by then she's forgotten all about it."

For the most part the students were well-behaved, but I had my share of class clowns. We had a clock in the front of the room that made a soft clicking sound each time the minute hand moved. One time I noticed that all the boys were looking eagerly at the clock and at one another. I could tell something was up. "Whatever you're planning to do at ten thirty, please don't do it," I admonished. They looked at one another glumly, and when ten thirty came nothing happened.

The next day at recess I asked one of the boys what they were planning to do. "We were going to lift the lids on our desks so you could only see the girls' faces," he replied. I realize now how innocent that seems compared to what they might try today.

One of my most challenging assignments was to have my eighth graders memorize fifty lines of poetry per month. They could memorize them all at once or split up the lines however they wanted as long as they finished fifty. I figured not only would that improve their memory skills, but it would foster a love of poetry they could carry with them the rest of their lives.

Once the poems were memorized, each student recited the lines in front of the class. A lot of kids were afraid of public speaking, but I didn't give them much of a choice. It was also a great listening exercise for the other students. Listening is a skill, too, and it has to be learned.

One time there was an announcement made that there would be no school the following Monday. My eighth graders acted like Mexican jumping beans the rest of the day. Finally I said to them, "You know what? I'm getting on your nerves, and you're getting on mine. So we're not going to talk to one another for the next half hour. You do your work, I'll do my work, and then we'll start all over." I sat at my desk, and we all worked quietly, and after thirty minutes, we started all over again with no problems at all.

I could be tough when I needed to be, but I never wanted to rule my classrooms through fear. I wasn't going to be one of those scary nuns. In fact, I've rarely met a scary nun. I know that's a major archetype, but I think it's a myth. Some of it came from the habits we wore. For some of the orders of sisters, the uniform included wearing leather straps, presumably to establish discipline, and I could see how that would be scary to a young child. But we never had leather straps in the BVM community.

One year my class had eighty-six students. Eighty-six! I learned to control the classroom by being stern but loving. If there's one thing I've discovered as a teacher, it's that fear is a bad motivator. I wanted the kids to think of me as a fun-loving kind of gal, habit and all. One day I heard chatter that they were trying to put together a

Saturday beach party—only, they were having a hard time finding a mother who could be a chaperone. I made a grand announcement. "I hear you're looking for a beach chaperone, and I'd be glad to do it!" They exchanged a few sideways glances.

Later in the afternoon I asked one of the boys, "So when are we leaving for the beach party?"

"We canceled it," he said.

Now, why wouldn't a bunch of teenage kids want to hang out with a nun on the beach?

Saint Charles had just about everything, but there was one glaring omission: sports. One day I went to the principal and asked if we could establish a program. She said we should take my request to the pastor. When we did, the pastor replied, "That will be fine, as long as you can take care of it."

"I'll take care of it," I assured him.

I was confident I could pull it off because I knew I would get a lot of help. Pretty soon we had a whole list of teams—boys and girls basketball, football, track, table tennis, and yo-yo. That's right, yo-yo was considered a sport back then, and the kids got to be pretty good at it. The Catholic Youth Organization (CYO) gave us substantial support. We belonged to a conference with other Catholic schools, and at the end of each season, all the schools would play in a big tournament.

I coached girls basketball. I also coached track, which was really easy to do. All I had to do was tell the kids to run, and off they went. Our football team didn't have any uniforms, so they wore jeans, and they didn't wear helmets. It was touch football, so it was pretty safe, although things could get quite rough at times.

Sometimes I would have the boys play the girls in basketball. I'd ask the boys to hold back a little bit, but we had some strong, athletic girls. Those games challenged them to improve and enhance their skills, as only sports can do. Our parents never complained about winning or losing. They were just happy their children were involved in something that was challenging and uplifting. That's much different from the squabbling you see today at youth soccer games. I've seen those soccer parents in action—they're fighters.

I thought I was a good basketball coach. I had watched the game, but I needed to learn more, so I read books about it. We practiced every day after school. We didn't win any tournaments, but the kids were very proud of themselves, and they had reason to be.

I also coached a girls softball team that qualified for the finals. We had an excellent pitcher, but on game day, she was so nervous that she was twitching her arm before each pitch, and the umpire kept calling balls. We lost the game, which was devastating for those kids.

I also ran the boys basketball practices, although we had a male coach for the games. One year we made it all the way to the semifinals of the conference playoffs, and everyone was so excited. The problem was that the game was scheduled for the same day as our school confirmation service. The students figured we wouldn't be able to play, but I couldn't let that happen. So I called the CYO and asked if they would change the start time. They told me that if the other school agreed, it was okay with them. I called the other school, and we got the game pushed back an hour.

As soon as the service was over, the players hustled out, changed out of their robes, and put on their gym clothes. I was sitting in a chair and looked up to see a pair of black pants standing next to me. It was Bishop Manning, and he was a little confused. I explained to him what was going on. The basketball team captain approached me and asked, "Do you think the bishop would bless the team?"

I told him to go ahead and ask, and Bishop Manning obliged us with a blessing. Then we went out and won the game. Coincidence? Maybe, maybe not.

One of my most important duties at Saint Charles was to help our eighth graders earn scholarships to the local private high schools. I was so busy during that first year just figuring out which end was up that I didn't put in the proper time, and the results reflected that. So in the second year I established a more structured program. We met in the mornings before school from eight to a quarter of nine. Then we worked on Saturday mornings from eight to eleven thirty. I wasn't paid extra to do this, nor did I ask to be. My reward was seeing my students reach their goals. Getting a scholarship meant drastically reducing the financial burden on those families.

This program really brought out my competitive spirit. There's nothing I love more than establishing a plan and working hard to meet—and beat—a challenge. I wanted to pass along that fire to my students. I wanted them to learn that there is no substitute for putting in extra time. We were so successful that some of the high schools complained that we were winning all the scholarships—they wanted those scholarships spread out equally. I thought that was unfair, since all we were doing was satisfying the requirements the school set. Nobody else was getting the results we were because nobody else was putting in the time. If the other schools had worked as hard as we did, they would have won more scholarships.

As if this wasn't a big enough workload, I was also put in charge of seventy altar boys. I had done this before at Saint Bernard's, but Saint Charles was a much bigger parish. We brought in twenty to thirty new altar boys each year, so I had to constantly train the new batch. Our priests conducted much of the services in Latin, so the boys had to learn the language well enough to understand what was happening. It was a massive responsibility. If any of the boys couldn't attend their assigned service, it was up to them to find a substitute.

Working with altar boys was incredibly special. It was so gratifying to see them rise to the occasion and accept all those duties. If they weren't attentive, it directly affected the service in a negative way. Being an altar boy was a purely volunteer effort, and for the most part, I think the boys enjoyed being there. They signed up because they wanted to serve their community, their church. A few of them went on to become priests themselves. I like to imagine that those formative days as altar boys brought them closer to God.

So, in a nutshell, I was teaching eighth grade for the first time, overseeing a sports program that I had created while coaching some of the teams, conducting a weekend scholarship program, and organizing the altar boys. You'd think my plate wasn't just full but overflowing. Yet I still found the time to pursue my English degree at Mount Saint Mary's University.

English became another specialty of mine, which came in handy because part of our mission at Saint Charles was to prepare the students for the annual California reading test. Those tests were crucial because they determined what level the students would take when they moved up to the next grade.

We had a memorable student at Saint Charles named Roger. One day when Roger was in the fifth grade, he told his mother he didn't feel well. She took him to the doctor, but they couldn't find anything wrong. Some time passed, and they eventually discovered that Roger had a brain tumor. He had to have surgery, and although he survived, he lost his eyesight.

He transferred into our school in the fifth grade. He had a good friend named Kenny Banks who sat next to him for every class and helped to pass along what I was teaching. Roger had a wonderful attitude and was very studious. At the end of the school year, he surprised me by asking if he could take the scholarship exam for Bellarmine-Jefferson High School. I called the principal and let her know I had a blind student who wanted to take the exam, and that he would need assistance. So she assigned a sister to read him the questions and write down his answers. Wouldn't you know it—Roger aced the exam and got the scholarship. We were all so thrilled for him!

Bob Hope's wife, Dolores, took a particular interest in Roger. She believed that if she visited and prayed at the Grotto of Our Lady of Lourdes in France and prayed for Roger, he would be cured of his blindness. Her sister suggested that instead of doing that, she should send Roger and his mother to the shrine. So that's what she did, and he regained about 10 percent of his eyesight back. Roger was at peace with what had happened to him, and he never let his disability hold him back. He ended up earning his PhD and taught at LA City College for many years.

We had another student in the eighth grade named Arlen who suffered from seizures because of a brain tumor. I trained the class so they would know exactly what to do in case he had a seizure. Arlen was an unbelievably artistic boy. One day while working on a project, he collapsed to the ground and had a seizure. Just as we had practiced, the students moved their desks out of the way so Arlen wouldn't injure himself. One of the girls ran to summon a priest, who came to the room and anointed him. Another went to the office so they could call for medical attention. Those steps helped Arlen get the help he needed, and within a few days he was back in school.

It always amazed me that Roger and Arlen knew how to handle their situations so well. They were very insistent that they did not want to be in a special school or any type of medical home. They wanted to learn right alongside the so-called normal kids. Those kids benefitted greatly from being in the same class as those two boys. They taught all of us lessons on a daily basis about the importance of staying strong, resilient, and optimistic in the face of extreme difficulty.

Getting children to learn is about much more than passing along the material. It's also important to know what motivates them and why. One year I had a student named Tommy. I knew he was intelligent, so I was confused when he performed poorly on the state test for reading. I asked him to meet me in my office before school one morning so we could discuss his situation. After some prodding, Tommy confessed that he intentionally scored poorly because he thought the work at the higher level would be too hard. I thought about this for a while and made a suggestion. "I have a group of seven boys and girls who need some help," I said. "They're going to be in your reading group, and it's going to be your responsibility to make sure they move up a level."

"Do you think I can do that?" he asked.

"I *know* you can," I replied. Sure enough, by the end of the school year, all the children were ready to move up a level, including Tommy.

Fast-forward about fifty years. I was working at Loyola, and our basketball coach, Jim Whitesell, told me that his brother lived in California and knew someone I had taught a long time ago. He told me the fellow's name: Tommy Maeder. Jim gave Tommy my information, and shortly thereafter I received a lovely letter from him.

Tommy did not include his phone number on the letter, so I looked it up in the white pages and dialed. (My younger readers will have to ask their parents—or maybe their grandparents—what the white pages were.) His wife answered the phone. I told her, "This is Sister Jean. I was Tommy's eighth-grade teacher." She got him right on the phone. Tommy informed me that he had become a certified teacher in California and had just retired from teaching eighth grade. It was gratifying to think that all those years ago I had given him that first inkling that he could be an excellent teacher.

Six

Principal Jean

When you love what you do, it
never really feels like work.

MY TENURE AT SAINT CHARLES marked my debut as a
TV star.

What, you think that only happened at the Final Four?

Our superiors at the archdiocese liked to stay ahead of all the
emerging trends. Television was becoming very popular in the mid-
1950s, and they wanted to find a way to involve our school in the
educational programming that was being broadcast with increasing
frequency. When they asked if I would teach a civics class on TV, I
readily agreed. Nobody ever accused me of being camera shy!

The class was supposed to be broadcast in the Channel 26 studio, which was at the University of Southern California. A couple
of days before the broadcast, however, there was a breakdown at

the studio, and there wasn't enough time to repair it. It looked like we were stuck, until I mentioned to the principal that Bob Hope's daughter Linda was in my class. I suggested we call her father and ask if he could provide a studio for us. The principal thought that was a splendid idea, and when we got ahold of Bob, he said it would be no problem. Such luck!

The next challenge was our attire. We were given strict instructions that we weren't allowed to wear anything white. The TV folks said that white fabric would bleed into the background. This was a problem because the trim on my habit around my face was white. So I had to dye that blue, and we did the same for the girls' blouses.

The big day came and we set up in the studio. When we went on the air, I didn't feel the least bit nervous. I was teaching my class, just as I did every day.

My mother traveled from San Francisco so she could watch us from inside the studio. The parents of the children in the class went around to all the local shops and asked them to turn the televisions in the windows to channel 26 so they could see the class. It was a small, early taste of celebrity for me. I could hardly have imagined the greater feast that was to come much later.

Oftentimes during my career I've heard teachers complain that their students weren't paying enough attention in class. I wanted to reply, "Well, maybe they'd pay better attention if you weren't so *boring*." I've always believed that it's the teacher's job to make learning easy and fun. If the students aren't learning, it's often the teacher's fault, not theirs.

Everything we did at the school was geared around this mind-set. When we taught the students about missions in California, we had them make clay models of the missions they were reading about. That engaged their imagination. When I taught eighth-grade math, I wrote a difficult problem on the board first thing in the morning. The students could work on the problem throughout the day whenever they were free, and then at the end of the day, we checked in to see who came up with the right answer. I made a game out of it.

When I taught geography, I didn't just drill into them the names of states and capitals. I encouraged them to explore other ways of life. I think this is so important. There are so many different cultures around the world, but we are all children of God. When you take the time to learn about other people in other places, it makes this very big world feel a bit smaller.

Each year during the national Catholic news reporter month, I tasked the students with writing an autobiography, just to get them thinking about writing. I made my corrections, and they revised the assignment. Afterward they kept the autobiography in a notebook with their other writings. I told them that they should hold on to those assignments just in case they were assigned the same topics in high school. Since it was authentically their own work, they were allowed to reuse them.

We used to say about our eighth graders: "They are neither fish nor flesh." They're not babies, but they're not fully formed adults either. They're grown up, but they're not grown-ups.

They're being forced to make a lot of decisions, but they don't always have the requisite maturity of judgment. When they made a mistake, our task wasn't to condemn them but rather encourage them to understand why they had chosen wrongly so they wouldn't do so again.

Eighth grade is about the time the boys start noticing the girls, and vice versa. It became a problem sometimes in the school because the boys would pass notes to the girls in class. I think the boys thought if they could show a girl that they liked her enough to pass a note and break a rule, then that would impress her.

One time I saw a note go across the aisle, and I snatched it up. I pinned it to my cape and wore it all day so everyone could see it. The boy just about fainted. I didn't look at the note until I got home. It was nothing, really, only his phone number. But I made my point, both to him and all the other students.

My number one piece of advice to aspiring teachers is to be honest with your students. If you don't know the answer to something, just say so. Whenever someone asked a question that stumped me, I would say, "Gosh, I don't know. Why don't we try to find the answer together?" If you pretend to know something you don't, the students will see through that right away. There's no use trying to fool them. It won't work.

Come to think of it, that's a good idea for all of our relationships. If you want to build trust with another person, the best way is to be honest with each other. Sometimes the truth can be a little embarrassing, but the trust gained from being honest makes it all worth it.

I had many, many students who went on to enjoy great success and even renown. But few students achieved such high success as a bright, young eighth-grade boy named Roger Mahony. He was the classic American boy, wo had a twin brother, and loved playing baseball. Roger dedicated himself to the religious life. He attended seminary in Fresno and was eventually made a bishop. On the week that Roger was elevated to the bishopric, I was in Denver attending an academic accreditation conference. I left the conference for a day so I could fly to Fresno and attend Roger's elevation ceremony.

I also attended the ceremony when Roger was made archbishop of Los Angeles in July 1985. But the greatest honor was when he was made a cardinal. That ceremony took place in Rome on June 28, 1991. That was right when Mundelein College had affiliated with Loyola University, and I was due to move into my new office. I called the provost and said I would not be able to be there on moving day because I was going to Rome to see my former eighth-grade student become a cardinal. The provost's wife had a connection that allowed me to stay in the Rome Center for twelve dollars a night—my friends were paying $200 to stay at a hotel down the street.

I beamed with pride as Roger became a cardinal. I had never been to Rome before, and the ceremony was beautiful. His mother was there, and we had a contingent from Los Angeles witnessing the big event. Cardinal Mahony served more than twenty years in Los Angeles before retiring in 2011. He now lives in a small house behind Saint Charles Church in North Hollywood. We continue to exchange Christmas and birthday cards. I'm extremely proud of all that he accomplished in helping serve God.

I spent my summers with many of my fellow sisters attending higher education classes at Loyola Marymount University. There was plenty of studying to do, but we still made time for fun. Our favorite activity was to go to the beach on Saturdays. The priests at LMU set up a bus so all of us could go. At the beach, there were favorite rocks where we hung out as the waves crashed around us. We had to wear our habits, so it's not like we could swim or go suntanning, but it was still a lovely time. Then we'd return to the campus where the priests organized a big barbecue for us.

Another fun activity was swimming. We used a swimming pool on campus. We had our own dressing rooms; everything had to be private because we were not permitted to be seen out of our habits in public, and certainly not in our bathing suits.

Summer was a great time to visit my family in the Bay Area. By this time both of my brothers were married and had families of their own. We still had the family ark, and we would all get together to spend a few days there, eating and hiking and swimming and having a merry old time. I took my nieces and nephews to the park and played with them for hours. They acted like I was so old. I'd try to teach them simple but fun games like kick the can and "one foot off the gutter," and they'd crack, "Is that what you did in the olden days, Aunt Dolores?"

When we were together and I wanted to swim, since I wasn't allowed to be seen out of my habit, my nieces and nephews had to stay inside when I went for a dip. My mother tipped me off that they huddled by a window so they could sneak a peek of me in a bathing suit and swim cap. I only hope they weren't too disappointed!

My summer higher education classes were a delight. I met all kinds of different sisters, and Loyola Marymount had a beautiful campus. I never felt stressed. I've always had a love for learning, and I knew that the time I was putting in would make me a better teacher and therefore help me feel more connected to my students. That connection was like oxygen to me. I craved it all the time and still do.

I chuckle to myself when people tell me they're stressed. I tell them, "Just wait 'til you get a few more years on your bones. You'll learn to go with the flow." Maybe they figure if a one-hundred-year-old lady isn't all that twisted, they could lighten up a bit too. Life's too short to be stressed all the time.

With all teaching and schooling, I didn't have many opportunities for downtime and hobbies, but I found ways to keep myself energized and entertained. Reading was a favorite hobby. As a child I read the Bobbsey Twins and Nancy Drew mysteries. I always knew someone in the neighborhood who had books from those series, so we'd exchange them all the time. The schools where I worked had libraries, so I checked out novels, especially mystery novels. I lost count of how many Agatha Christie books I read.

With so many people in the movie business in our community, we had no problem getting access to feature films. The school had a projector that we were permitted to take back to our convent on weekends. One time a parent from our school sent us thirteen reels and said they had to get back to the studio, so we spent all weekend watching them. There was another group of sisters in Santa Ana who also had connections, but the trip was forty miles one way. So we'd meet one of them at a gas station halfway between us and exchange film cans. I remember one time our superior got a copy of the movie *Lost Horizon*. I think I watched that seven times. We also loved classic movies like *Singin' in the Rain* and *Citizen Kane*.

I also enjoyed listening to the radio that sat on a shelf behind my bed. The first television I remember watching regularly was in the 1950s when I was living at the convent. We had one very small TV, and we mostly watched religious programs on it.

Sports was another favorite pastime. I enjoyed talking to the sisters about what was going on in football, baseball, and other sports. That's when I came to discover the NCAA men's basketball tournament. This was long before anyone called it March Madness or used the term *Final Four*. It was also long before anyone knew what "bracketology" was. But we knew all about it, and we filled out our own brackets together to see who could pick the games the best. We'd wait until all the West Coast games were over so we could post the results the next morning on a bulletin board. That's how news traveled in the olden days.

Other than that, I guess you could say I was a workaholic, although I enjoyed my work so much that I never thought of myself that way. This was one of many behaviors I learned from my parents. When my dad worked for the city of San Francisco all those years, he came home at the end of the day for dinner and then went to work for a few hours in the evening. He actually had to retire six months early because he had earned so much overtime. Even after he retired, my dad kept right on working part-time for the police department. He was put on a security detail that protected the archbishop's home when he believed they were under threat. My dad was an extrovert, and he loved that job. He spent evening after evening just walking the neighborhood and talking to people.

My mom was much the same way. One of her favorite expressions was, "It's better to wear out than rust out." She was always moving around the house, making cookies and cooking and organizing her children's lives. Maybe this wasn't a "job" per se, but it was a lot of work. Although when you love what you do, it never really feels like work.

In 1955, I was given a new assignment as principal at Saint Brendan School in Los Angeles. I was excited for the opportunity but also sad to say goodbye to Saint Charles. Between the students, their parents, my fellow sisters, and the rest of the community, I had made so many friends. But I had gotten my marching orders from the BVM community, and that was that.

I moved into a convent that housed ten sisters who taught at two different schools. That year also brought about a major change for us—we were granted permission to drive. I had originally gotten my driver's license at the age of seventeen, and at that time California gave lifetime licenses, so I was ready to resume driving immediately. We had a house car that all the sisters used to commute to work, and the parish provided us with other cars as well. It made life a lot more convenient, that's for sure.

I knew I had much to learn to become an effective principal, but this time I felt ready. My dad gave me great advice at the outset. "If your pastor tries to run your school," he said, "you tell him that you are trained for this and he is not."

The school had an enrollment of approximately four hundred students, but our building was a mess. It was thirty years old and badly in need of repairs. Then we were informed that it was also a fire hazard. There had been a tragic fire at one of our schools in Chicago, and as a result the fire department came in and inspected all our schools. They said if we didn't come up with a plan to reduce the number of people in the classrooms, we would have to close down the school.

Welcome to your new job, Madam Principal! I immediately gathered the faculty, and we came up with a plan to break up the school day into two different sessions. The first set of students came in from 8 a.m. until noon, and then the second attended classes from 12:30 p.m. to 4:30 p.m. It was quite difficult because we were reluctant to hire any more teachers. Money was tight, and we were concerned about bringing in people who were unfamiliar with our school. It made for very long days—there was no more recess, unfortunately—but we had no other choice.

Eventually we were able to build a new school with two stories. However, we couldn't use the upper floor for any of the younger ones because their little legs couldn't go down those stairs fast enough to escape a fire. So I moved my class into a garage on our property. We were only allowed forty-nine children in that space, but the class had fifty, so one student had to sit in a back doorway. I called that student a floater, because if someone was absent that day he could step into the "classroom" and occupy the empty seat. Eventually we figured out a way to make it work so everyone could be in school the entire day, from 8:30 a.m. to 2:30 p.m.

On top of my principal duties, I also taught a full slate of eighth-grade classes. I used the auditorium, and because it was the largest room in the building, I often accommodated overflow students. One of my students was a boy named Michael Mullen—who later joined the navy, became a highly decorated war veteran, and eventually rose to the position of chairman of the joint chiefs of staff under Presidents George W. Bush and Barack Obama. Michael and I lost touch over the years, but after I gained notoriety at Loyola, he visited me at my residence.

As a principal, I also had to deal with discipline issues. On one occasion I was called in to handle a delicate situation. It appeared that someone—presumably an altar boy—was stealing money from the collection basket we passed around during Sunday mass. I was asked to help find out who it was. Another teacher and I observed the children in the classroom one morning. We told them what was happening and that we wanted to talk to each of them. One boy asked the other teacher to go to the bathroom, and she said no. A little while later, she saw him standing by a cabinet and noticed that he dropped something out of his pocket. He didn't realize she had seen him.

Clearly, we found the culprit. Instead of coming down hard on him, I wanted to handle it with love and try for a teaching moment. I sat down with the boy, and he confessed to everything. I told him to call his father and ask him to come to school after work. When the father heard what his son had done, he was devastated. It took a long time for the boy's mother to get over it, too, but he wasn't expelled from school. The pastor asked him to do extra chores around the church for a while. I do think the boy was ashamed at what he had done. We never had trouble with him again.

There were also many fun times at the school. Saint Brendan had a lovely playground but no sports program. We quickly remedied that. Within a few months, we had a variety of teams organized. Because I was principal I didn't have time to do any coaching, but the sisters on the faculty were happy to assist. I went to all the games, which was sometimes challenging because different teams often played at the same time.

I also started a school band. We hired an instructor from Bellarmine-Jefferson in Burbank to establish it. The children became so good that they played for our flag salute in the morning and for our dismissal in the afternoon. They also got to march in the Fourth of July parade in Burbank.

The 1960 elections were a big deal in our community, not least because John F. Kennedy was attempting to become our first Catholic president. It confused, amazed, and disappointed me that this was even an issue. People had funny ideas, such as worrying that Kennedy would get his directions from the pope if he became president. That seemed like such a childish thing, but apparently many people believed it.

I wanted to use the excitement of the election to get our students engaged. We decided to have our own votes with the seventh and eighth graders. We gave everybody a copy of the exact ballot that would be decided on Election Day. The students were asked to vote on every single office and ballot measure, not just who they wanted for president. We had debates leading up to the voting so the students could hear all sides of the arguments. Everyone had to "register" to vote, and a couple of our international students served as poll watchers. The voting took place in our bookstore. I'm telling you, we were very, very serious about this whole thing. It was a great civics lesson.

We held our own vote the day before Election Day. We spent all afternoon tallying up the votes on a big chalkboard. It turned out that our results were almost exactly the same as the way Los Angeles voted as a whole.

Being a principal was my first chance to be a "boss." That's not my natural pose, but I grew into the job. I always understood that the key to being a successful principal is to have a competent faculty, and I knew I had that. I had two lay teachers and the rest were sisters, and they were all terrific. It's a lot like coaching basketball: you're only as good as your players. I may have been new to the job, but I knew right away that I was part of a winning team.

When I moved to Saint Brendan in 1955, I was told it would be a six-year appointment. By the time those six years were over, I had earned my master's degree in education. During the summer of 1961, I was visiting with sisters at the pool at Loyola Marymount when I received a call from our house saying that my new orders had arrived. The sister brought the letter to the university. I learned that I was being sent to Mundelein College, an all-women's school in Chicago, to teach in their education department.

Me? A college teacher? I was taken aback. What would I ever do there?

I assumed I would be working at another elementary or middle school somewhere in Los Angeles. I had never taught in college before, so I felt woefully unprepared. I was sad to leave my friends in California and especially sad to be moving so far from my family, although my parents assured me we would visit each other plenty. As in all the prior cases, I understood in the end that I had chosen this life and this mission, and that each move would bring uncertainty but also great promise.

Once again, I had no choice but to go with the flow. Life's too short to be stressed, right? I packed up my belongings and flew to Chicago, where I was met at the airport by a representative from Mundelein and taken to my new home. Whatever was going to happen, I trusted that God had a plan for me. It was my duty as His servant to trust His judgment and carry it out.

Seven

Mundelein

We need to be at least a little
uncomfortable in order to grow.

IT HAD BEEN TWENTY years since my brief tenure in Chicago as a fresh-faced rookie teacher at Saint Vincent's school. My face may not have been quite so fresh, but my spirit was still young. The city hadn't changed much—it was still vibrant and hopeful, full of culture and energy, resplendent in the spring and brutally cold in winter—but I knew I had changed. My return engagement was not a blast from the past so much as a renewal and reinvention as a college professor. Mundelein hired me to be a teacher, but I had a lot to learn.

Mundelein was an iconic school that rose literally out of the ashes. The official groundbreaking ceremony occurred three days after the stock market crash of 1929. The BVM community pressed on through the Depression and erected an institution that has honored our mission of service, education, humility, and inclusion. Named for Chicago's archbishop, Cardinal Mundelein, the school offered a curriculum that combined traditional liberal arts (philosophy, economics, literature, etc.) with practical life skills. I was hired as part of a growth wave occurring under Sister Mary Ann Ida Gannon, who had been hired as president six years before my arrival.

In all, there were eighty sisters on the faculty. I had never lived with that many sisters before. We had private rooms, although to call them "rooms" might be generous since each one was about the size of a closet. That didn't bother me one bit. Everyone was warm and welcoming, and I was excited to write a brand-new chapter.

It helped that I already knew the chairman of the education department, Sister Margaret, because she had been two years ahead of me at the motherhouse in Dubuque. She gave me a heavy course load right off the bat. I was assigned to teach philosophy of education, and I had two sections of reading methods and two sections of math methods. The math classes were especially challenging because the new math was starting to work its way into the curriculum. I had to attend a seminar every week to get up to speed.

There was a lot of controversy about the "new math." The idea was to force students to give more thought as to why they were applying the numbers a certain way. It was complicated, and the teachers had to attend workshops in order to learn it. I went along and did my job, but I also had my way of explaining things that offered shortcuts and made problems a little easier to understand. Frankly, I thought it was a little silly that some company was trying to make teachers explain math to their students, considering most of us were already doing that.

I always thought the most important thing was to make math—or any subject—fun. It *is* possible, you know. For instance, we used to start our classes by asking students to do seventy-two math combinations in two minutes as fast as they could. They might start off taking seven minutes, but after a while they could get it down to two.

I also tagged along with one of the nuns and observed her as she conducted her tour of Chicago public schools. That was especially important because teaching young women to be schoolteachers in Chicago was a big part of our mission. I enjoyed that experience because it allowed me to be around young kids, which always made me so happy.

Although the material in college was different, the method was the same: repeat, repeat, repeat. It's the only way to assure true understanding.

Sister Ann Ida was a magnificent leader with fantastic drive and imagination, and she was a ubiquitous presence around the city. She served on a lot of important boards, where she was often the first woman to join. Our student body included approximately 150 young nuns who lived in a brick building eleven stories high that we called the Scholasticate. It was our house of studies. The nuns had spent time as postulants at the motherhouse in Dubuque, made their vows, and come right to Chicago to pursue their degrees at Mundelein. In December their director got sick, so they asked me to come and help them prepare for Christmas. That led to me being appointed as assistant director of the Scholasticate. I just loved being around those sisters. They were like younger versions of me.

I was in my forties by then, but I never had any problem relating to young people—I still don't! Some were having issues with their families, who resisted the idea of their being sisters, so I helped them work through that. As far as I was concerned, I was there for whatever they needed, which is why we were able to bond so quickly. Once someone senses you are truly invested in their dreams, they come to trust you and gravitate toward you. That's the blessed life of a teacher.

Once I became assistant director of the Scholasticate, I had to oversee a lot of the logistical operations. I served as treasurer of the house and was responsible for working with the kitchen people on planning meals and following a budget. We didn't have maids, so I had to check to make sure the residents were performing all their house duties. And I didn't just tell them what to do—I helped them do it. We shared the responsibilities, which brought us even closer.

In time, I developed a reputation as a Johnny-on-the-spot (Jean-on-the-spot?) plug-in for a variety of situations. Got a minor problem that needs a quick fix? Let Sister Jean take a whack at it. In the spring of '62, for example, there arose a problem with Mundelein's graduation. All the seniors were trying to practice lining up for the ceremony, but the situation became chaotic. I happened to walk into the room, and there was all kinds of noise. Some of the girls were crying because it wasn't coming together, and the sister in charge of the event was complaining that the girls weren't properly getting into line. I thought to myself, *Oh, gee, that's a surprise, girls not wanting to get in line.*

They asked me to help. As I looked over her instructions, I realized they were complicated and unfocused. This issue went back to my central axiom as a teacher: if the students aren't learning, it's your fault, not theirs. So I simplified the instructions, explained them to the students as clearly as I could, encouraged them through their mistakes with humor and compassion, and put them through their paces. When graduation day came, the ceremony went off without a hitch. I guess my superiors thought I had done a great job, because they put me in charge of graduation line-up for the next thirty years.

Not surprisingly, I gravitated toward the sports teams. Mundelein had a volleyball team, and it wasn't long before I was drafted into driving the girls to away games. All the schools in our division were in our area, so we didn't have to travel too far. I liked being around those players and loved their matches, although one time we did get a flat tire on the way home. I managed to coax the car into a gas station so it could be fixed. I called the house to assure the sisters that the game hadn't gone into overtime and we would be home shortly.

On another occasion, I drove the team through a bad snowstorm. When we got to the game, we learned that the referees couldn't make it. I offered to serve as a replacement. Both teams agreed, and we had the match. I can't imagine something like that happening today.

Mundelein's campus was located right next to the campus of Loyola University. We even shared a fence. So we followed with particular interest the journey of the 1962–63 Loyola men's basketball team. The Mundelein women played the Loyola women in basketball, and oftentimes those games were followed by the men's games, so I got to see a few of them in person. The Ramblers won twenty-one games before suffering their first loss. It was all very exciting, and we continued to follow the team as they made their way through the NCAA tournament. I vividly remember watching the championship game against Cincinnati on the TV set that belonged to a brother-in-law of one of the Mundelein sisters, Sister Joan Therese. It was an eleven-and-a-half-inch black-and-white set. The game had already been completed by the time it came on TV—they called it a "tape delay"—but nobody told us the outcome, so it was still suspenseful. As soon as the game ended, we heard all these voices coming down Sheridan Road.

That championship wasn't just exciting, it was also historic. Back then there was an unwritten rule in college basketball that a team should not have more than two Black players in the game at the same time. Loyola's coach, George Ireland, regularly played three or four Black players. The team made the NCAA tournament, but once they got to the second round, they encountered a problem. Their opponent was supposed to be Mississippi State, but in Mississippi there was another unwritten rule that white players were not supposed to play with or against Black players. When the Mississippi State president said he would send the team to Michigan to play the game, several state politicians tried to prevent them from leaving. So the team literally had to sneak out of the state to play the game, which Loyola won, 61–51.

That has come to be referred to as "the Game of Change." It's an inspiring story because it reminds all of us of the power of sports to bring people together through all kinds of barriers. One of the best parts about basketball is that the ball doesn't know the race of the hand that shoots it. If the arc is true, the ball goes in.

And yet, at the time I don't remember anyone remarking upon

the racial history that was being made by that team. It wasn't until later that I was able to appreciate the greater championship that was won that year. We also learned a lot more about what those players went through with the unkind remarks and racist hate mail they received. It was jarring and upsetting to learn those details, but it was crucial that everyone heard the truth.

I can't say this for certain, but I would bet that many Black people who followed that team were very aware that the Ramblers were making history. Me? I thought I was watching a basketball game. This speaks to the reality that for far too long Black people and white people have lived a separate existence in this country, with whites' circumstances usually being much more privileged. That is just a fact. When I reflect on my childhood as well as my experiences as a teacher in Southern California, I remember thinking we had a diverse community, but the truth is, in all my years at the three private Catholic schools where I taught in California, we did not have a single Black student. That is simply wrong and grossly unfair.

Things changed over time, spurred on by the Supreme Court's landmark ruling in the *Brown vs. Board of Education* case. That decision was handed down ninety years after the Civil War ended. It highlights our very little progress since the end of that war. We've done better, but clearly we have a long way to go to achieve racial equity. One of the problems we face is that people are so emotional when it comes to racism (and understandably so) that they end up shouting and arguing with one another instead of listening and reasoning with one another. That results in people talking only to people who are like them and agree with them. The classroom is often a much better environment for people to discuss their different perspectives, work out their differences, and try to reach some kind of consensus.

I've seen so many instances in my life of this kind of prejudice and bigotry. I pray for people who feel this way. I know they have love in their hearts, and I ask God to release it for them. I realize that it's human nature to be afraid of things that are unfamiliar or people who may look different or come from a different background. But Jesus taught us to love one another no matter what our differences— indeed, *because* of our differences. I really believe that if we could just see one another the way God sees us, this kind of nonsense would never take place.

I really don't understand people who want to whitewash history and insist that schoolteachers don't inform their students of the unpleasant realities of our past. People are fallible, and our country, while great, is far from perfect. If we don't learn about our mistakes, how will we learn *from* them?

Later that year in November, while teaching a class the dean at Mundelein made an announcement, asking the entire school to make their way into the auditorium. We didn't know the reason, so we were naturally concerned as we dropped everything and headed down the hallways. Once we were assembled, the dean took to the stage and announced, "I'm afraid I have some very bad news. The president has been shot." There was a huge cry and emotional response because many of us thought she was referring to the president of Mundelein, Sister Ann Ida Gannon, who was in Washington, DC, attending a higher-education meeting. Several of the students started sobbing. The dean soon realized the misunderstanding, so she clarified that she was talking about President Kennedy.

Like everyone else in that room and around the world, I was shocked to hear the news. I thought about Jackie and how their two adorable children would have to grow up without knowing their father. We all felt like we really knew them personally. Looking back, I guess I was pretty naïve, thinking something like that wouldn't ever happen. Although other presidents had been assassinated, it just didn't seem possible that it could happen again. Many historians have pointed to the Kennedy assassination as the moment when America lost its innocence. I think there's a lot of truth to that. If anything, things have gotten much, much worse in this respect when it comes to violence in our society in general.

By this time, I was pretty much done with my outside schooling. I had plenty of work trying to stay up-to-date. That included a new role as the director of summer sessions. The work started the previous Christmas as I canvassed our faculty and determined what everyone wanted to teach. I also oversaw the residence arrangements for the students and teachers, many of whom were visiting priests and nuns. I put an emphasis on evening dances and other social activities, as well as trips around the city. I knew people, especially young people, wouldn't just want to spend their summers working all day and night. They needed to have fun too.

The only downside was that the job was so all-encompassing that I didn't have time to do any teaching myself over the summer. There was so much to do in making sure students were on track for their graduation requirements. Students came into my office all the time, and when they weren't in my office, I walked around campus to visit with them and see how they were doing.

One of the dangers of having to meet so many short-term deadlines is that we tend to stop innovating and growing. In her first year as president, Sister Ann Ida created Mundelein's first-ever theology department. In 1962 she initiated a broad self-study that was conducted by a lay person named Dr. Norbert Hruby, one of the leading experts at institutional analysis. Dr. Hruby's mission was to help us take a good look at ourselves and map out a plan for the future. He talked to our students, faculty, administrators, and alumni. He also empowered everyone to be a part of the process. That way nobody felt threatened.

Dr. Hruby helped us to form committees, and all of us were assigned to areas in which we were not familiar—everyone had to learn something new. I was put on the library committee, which was perfect because I knew almost nothing about how our library was run. We visited several other college libraries, including the one at Notre Dame, to get a sense of what was happening elsewhere. We determined that Mundelein needed a much bigger library than the one we had, so we wrote a grant proposal that earned us $1 million in public funds to fuel an expansion.

Dr. Hruby wrote a report that offered various suggestions. The biggest change was moving from a semester system to a term system. Each term lasted ten weeks, which required us to make classes longer. We also launched a groundbreaking Degree Completion Program, which allowed women who had left school before graduating to come back and finish. Those classes began at 10 a.m. and finished at 2 p.m. This allowed the women with younger kids to drop them off at school in the morning and pick them up afterward. We had to be very selective about who we chose to teach those classes. We focused on teachers who had PhDs in adult learning. This followed a very important rule in education: the teacher has to fit the students, rather than forcing the students to fit the teacher.

Whether it's a coach, a teacher, a business executive, or any other kind of leader, I believe it's vital that the person in charge understands the people who are working for him or her and to ensure that the job never becomes stale. This might mean making people uncomfortable at times, but that's okay. We need to be at least a little uncomfortable in order to grow. I've always tried to remember that when faced with change and to trust that God's plan will work out in the end.

This being the 1960s, there were really big changes happening in America and around the world. In our world of the BVM community, we were dealing with significant changes as a result of the Second Vatican Council, also known as Vatican II. This was a series of meetings that took place in Rome from 1962 to 1965. Pope John XXIII formed the council because he believed the Catholic Church needed to be updated to stay better connected with the twentieth-century population. The world was becoming more secular, and though the Catholic Church is not normally known for its willingness to change, the pope wisely understood that we can be flexible in ways that are productive without moving off our core values.

One of the big changes to come out of Vatican II was that Catholic orders were no longer required to have nuns and sisters wear habits. They didn't force anyone to stop wearing habits, but they did give us the option. This was big news in my world. Most everyone, including me, decided to stop wearing the habit and wear contemporary clothes. I must say we all looked pretty tacky for a while. We had a lot to learn about modern fashion! One of the benefits of wearing a habit is that you don't have to bother shopping for clothes. Years later we looked back at old photos and laughed at how silly we dressed. Fortunately, my tastes have evolved over time.

I preferred not to wear a habit, partly because I thought it contributed to the image of sisters as very strict and worthy of fear. I never minded the habit, but I was perfectly happy to switch to contemporary clothes. Besides being more comfortable, I thought it would help people relate to us better. I thought about all those airline flights I took to visit my family in San Francisco. When someone would sit next to me, it seemed they would get nervous and not want to talk to me. Or maybe the opposite happened, and they wanted to talk the entire flight. I'd get all kinds of reactions. I remember one time someone said to me, "I'm glad you're here, because if something happens to this plane you'll be able to save us." I smiled and said, "The pilot sits up front. I think he'll be the one to save us."

Here's another thing people don't realize about nuns' habits: they retain the smell of smoke. If we were in a public space where people were smoking, it would take many washings to get rid of the smell, and sometimes it would never rinse out.

Vatican II gave us more freedom to do other things as well. People could now invite us to their homes or to a restaurant and see the good we were trying to do. Amid all this change, the BVMs in Chicago hosted a huge conference that was attended by about 1,300 sisters. I was given a major role in the planning, including registration and accommodations at the Congress Hotel. Everyone was asked to fill out a survey in advance of the conference. This was 1968, remember, so the data had to be collected the old-fashioned way. The surveys arrived by mail, and we had to organize, collate, and tabulate everyone's answers. It was fascinating work but also time-consuming.

The best part of this process was that the sisters were given a much bigger role in decision-making than they'd ever had before. We were asked for our opinions, and we broke off into various committees and subgroups to flesh out our ideas. This was another reflection of Vatican II. Women had not been participants in some of the early meetings, but when this was pointed out to Pope Paul, he invited at least a dozen women to become official auditors.

One change that Vatican II did not make—and that the church still hasn't made—was to invite women into the priesthood. If the pope decided to take this step, I would be supportive of his judgment, but it has never bothered me that only men are allowed to become Catholic priests. We think of certain positions as more powerful and prestigious, but I don't think God sees us that way. I think we are all equal in His eyes. In biblical times all the apostles were men, and the women served them. Who's to say that puts the women in a lesser place? I believe it's our place to serve God.

I realize I sound hopelessly old-fashioned when I say these things. When I mention these notions to some of my female students, they often reply, "Sister Jean, you're crazy." That's okay, I don't mind. I love that they keep me young and that they still love talking to this old nun even though some of her beliefs are *so* last century.

Eight

War and Peace

Hope makes me happy.

THE TIMES THEY WERE a-changin'.

Like most every college in America, Mundelein was swept up by the tumult of the 1960s—the civil rights movement, the women's movement, the Vietnam War, and all the cultural changes that were happening. Not only was that unavoidable for us, it was preferable. It's not the job of a university to form a protective cocoon around its students so that they can focus solely on their studies. It's the university's job to make sure the students are connected to their community and their country. In many cases, that is the best way for them to learn who they are, what they believe, and who they want to become. Mark Twain said it best: "I have never let schooling interfere with my education."

Our students were particularly focused on racial justice. We were located in a northern, diverse city, and though we were not without racial tension, we were not segregated like so many southern states. Many of the students wanted to get involved in the protests that were taking place down South. Instead of discouraging them, we believed it was our job to help them participate safely.

For the most part, they were able to do so without incident, although we were rattled when a group of Mundelein students traveled to Selma, Alabama, in 1965 to march with John Lewis. That was the infamous incident where Lewis and other marchers were beaten by police as they tried to walk across the Edmund Pettus Bridge. Fortunately, our students were unharmed, but it was a disturbing reminder of how dangerous these activities could be.

I sympathized with the marchers and was a big supporter of the civil rights movement, but I didn't travel to Selma or anywhere down South. I believed my task was to facilitate activities on campus while listening to people on all sides, including those who disapproved of what was happening. Many of those people were likewise supportive of the idea of civil rights, but they didn't always appreciate the methods the students used. Regardless of what my own personal views were, I believed it was important that everyone on campus felt like they had a voice in this incredibly important discussion. Those led to difficult but healthy conversations. It was an unsettling time for everyone.

That's what made the 1969 moon landing so special. I'll never forget watching it unfold on a small black-and-white TV with my fellow sisters. Oh, was that something! To see all of that happening in real time on live television was mesmerizing and also quite scary. I was mostly relieved that the guys got there safely, because there was a lot of speculation that they might not.

The moon landing was a unifying moment for the country, but those good vibrations didn't last long. Our world was rocked on May 4, 1970, when four students at Kent State University were killed by members of the Ohio National Guard during a campus protest. As soon as news of the shooting spread, a large group of Mundelein students launched an impromptu protest on Sheridan Road, which was the busiest avenue near our campus. Someone took red paint and poured it on the statue of our two angels. Our facilities staff cleaned the statues before classes started the next day.

We held an emergency meeting of the faculty. Some suggested that we clear the campus and have the students work from home. Many teachers, including myself, thought that was a bad idea. We preferred to devise methods to help students engage in protests while staying up-to-date with their work. We asked each student to put in writing what her plan was so we could all be on the same page. This solution was consistent with our philosophy that it's the job of a school to empower its students rather than just setting standards and expecting the students to meet them no matter what. In these situations, the teachers have as much to learn from their students as the other way around.

A few older sisters at Mundelein were extremely opposed to the protests. They wanted those girls in the classroom, not shouting out on Sheridan Road. After Kent State, a few members of the faculty suggested we close down the college until the Vietnam War was over. Thank God we didn't take their advice. If we had closed down the school at that point, it might never have reopened.

To be sure, I did see some excesses. We had students who wanted to be away all the time marching for every cause under the sun. Activism is important, but if you're going to be enrolled in college, you have to meet your obligations if you expect to graduate.

I must say, I had mixed feelings about all the protesting. There is a time and place for civil disobedience, but the only way to create real, meaningful, lasting change is through quiet, persistent work. It means crafting well-thought-out proposals and then persuading people to come around to your way of thinking. Some of the students expected the college to give them everything they wanted, when it was our position that they should be part of any changes that were going to take place. And oftentimes they failed to recognize that there was disagreement among themselves over what changes needed to be made.

Personally, I was very opposed to the Vietnam War. I had a nephew who was drafted and served in the war, and after he came back, he was never the same. I don't believe there is any such thing as a just war. It's much better for opposing sides to find a way to negotiate their way through their problems, but people often don't want to do that because they are so entrenched in their positions. I see the same thing happening in politics. People hold to their beliefs and get so riled up about those who disagree with them that they end up talking over one another, and there are no constructive results.

I guess this is part of our flawed nature as human beings. Wars have been going on forever. If you read the Old Testament, there are so many stories about people killing one another for all kinds of reasons. As I said before, I pray for the day when there will be no war, and although I don't expect to live long enough to see that happen, I will never lose hope. Maybe I'm a Pollyanna, maybe I'm an eternal optimist, maybe I'm delusional. But I am who I am. Hope makes me happy.

Unlike many people, I actually flourish on change. I don't believe in change for change's sake, but if something needs to be reformed, then do it. It's good to be old-fashioned in some respects, but it's also important to have common sense.

As I wrote earlier, I believe my adaptability is my superpower. I think a major reason why I have this outlook is the nature of religious life. When I entered the BVM community, I understood that it was my duty to go wherever I was sent and serve God with good cheer and to the best of my ability. It was always heart-wrenching when I had to leave one place to go to another and say goodbye to so many people I cared about very deeply. But the upside to that was that I didn't just learn to adapt to change—I expected it.

At first, when I arrived at a new place, I would say to myself, "Now don't get too attached to these people. You're going to have to leave them at some point." But of course that was unavoidable. I love people, and I naturally became quite close with my students as well as with my fellow sisters who were serving the same mission as I was.

All of this prepared me for the tumult of the sixties and seventies. The students weren't championing for changes only in the South. They wanted to make things better at home too. They prodded the faculty and administration at Mundelein to diversify our curriculum and our student population. As a result, we formed an organization called MuCuba, a Black students association. We also brought more Black culture and Black history into our academic curriculum, which I agreed was much needed. The classes were filled with white and Black students, and some of the men from

Loyola attended as well. The students also asked for a Black theology class. It was difficult to find the right teacher, but we finally did in Sister Teresita, who was a Black nun and a wonderful instructor. She was tough, but the students really responded to her. She went on to be active in many organizations around the city. We were lucky to have her.

On top of these changes, we hired a new vice president for academic affairs, who helped us do a thorough institutional analysis. Every student, alumna, and faculty member was asked to fill out a lengthy questionnaire and give ideas on how the curriculum could be improved, not just for Black students but for everybody. I was an acting dean at the time, so I was involved in a lot of those discussions. It was a challenging time, but I was proud that the people who ran Mundelein were so open to new ideas. That's what higher education should be about.

This became part of a broader conversation the students wanted to have about our curriculum. Rather than blowing off those concerns or making changes ourselves, we invited them into the process. We held a curriculum conference, heard all points of view, and instituted changes we hoped would meet their desires. One of the changes was to allow students more choice about what classes would be required to get their degrees. We did that for a few years, but after the students graduated, many of them expressed disappointment over the results. They recognized that being allowed to completely pick and choose their classes wasn't the best decision in the end. They felt as if they had missed out on too much. What they learned was that it's all well and good to study electives and areas of specific interest, but it's also important to study the humanities.

Even if you only get a taste, sometimes it's enough to make you want to learn more.

A big part of the student protest movement focused on women's rights. As a woman teaching at an all-women's college, I was especially intent on following this conversation. Once again, I found myself conflicted. On the one hand, I understood that women were being denied access to opportunities, especially jobs, that were being made available only to men. That wasn't right. On the other hand, I felt some of the feminists were going too far. I don't think someone should get a job or be elected to political office simply because she's a woman. It doesn't do anybody any good if they are hired into a position for which they are not qualified.

Many years later, I likewise felt that too many people argued that Hillary Clinton should be president just because she was a woman. I voted for Hillary because I thought she was intelligent and had high principles, not because she was a woman. I realize this may sound old-fashioned (again), but I believe everybody should be judged equally. We have a long way to go to get there.

Some people on our campus argued that Mundelein should become a coed school, but that idea didn't gain much traction. We were already next-door neighbors to Loyola, so it's not as though there weren't opportunities for our students to make male friends. We had a great number of marriages between students who went to Mundelein and Loyola. Many of us thought it would be a better business model to distinguish ourselves from the other coed schools. If we were an all-male school making the change it would have been a different story, but I simply did not think we could recruit enough men to make it work. Going coed would have put us in competition with a lot more schools, and there's a good chance we wouldn't have fared as well. Our numbers were already going down considerably. Making that kind of change would have been our death knell.

In 1974 I became director of Coffey Hall, a residence hall that housed two hundred women. In past years they had appointed someone to that position, but in 1974 leadership allowed the students to choose their director. That meant going through an interview process. Up to that point, the women had known me only as an academic advisor working in the dean's office. I guess I interviewed well enough, because they accepted my appointment.

It was the first time I was going to live with students rather than with nuns. I was fifty-three years old at the time, but it never occurred to me that I was too old. I had as much energy as any college student—and still do!

The upshot of this move was that it made my days that much longer. I worked in the dean's office until seven at night and then went over to the residence hall. I visited all four floors and knocked on everyone's door to make sure they were okay. One winter we had sixty people down with the flu. I told everyone to stay out of one another's rooms until it was gone. I brought the girls orange juice and pampered them every night until they got better. I was lucky I never got sick.

For a long time, the drinking age in Illinois was eighteen, but in 1961 the age increased to twenty-one. But try telling that to our students! We knew they wanted to drink and that it was against the law. As a director of a residence hall, it was up to me to enforce this, but I can't say I was much of an enforcer. The reality was that college kids were going to drink. As long as things didn't get out of hand, we had our own gentleman's agreement that this was to be out of sight, out of mind.

It's not that I approved of their drinking, but I didn't want to waste energy and good will. I'd walk down the hallways at night and hear someone say very loudly, "Good evening, Sister Jean." I knew that was a message to the other students to put away their bottles. They thought they were pulling a fast one on ole Sister Jean. I actually had a few of the former students from Coffey Hall visit me at Loyola recently, and we had a good laugh when I told them I had known exactly what they were doing.

As it happens, I moved into Coffey Hall just as there was a big debate over visitation hours. This was another impending change that forced us to adjust to the students as opposed to the other way around. As a school, we had to recognize that our students naturally wanted more time to receive male visitors. Some of the parents didn't like the idea of young men visiting their daughters late at night, so we set aside one floor where the visiting hours didn't change. Visitors had to sign in and be escorted into the building by their hostess. I met a lot of the boys, and we got along fine. If they were uncomfortable with the idea of an old nun living in the residence hall, they didn't let it show. Gradually we extended the visitation time, although we never got to a point where male visitors were allowed to stay all night. That would definitely have been a leap too far.

Nowadays, of course, we have women and men living on the same floor of their residence hall. When people ask me how I feel about that, I tell them I'm perfectly fine with it. I often tell the story of when I was living in Creighton Hall, which is coed, at Loyola. I asked the girls one time how they liked living next to the guys. They said they liked it because the boys were computer majors, so if the girls had any issues with their computers, the boys were right there to help.

Around this time I took a trip to Kansas State University as part of my work on an evaluation committee for accrediting schools. A group of students asked if I would join them for breakfast. We arrived early, so we were the only ones in the cafeteria. When I asked what this meeting was about, a student replied, "We heard that Mundelein just went to extended visitation hours, and we want to know how you did that."

They took copious notes as I recounted how it all unfolded. Then I had them read the notes back to me. I told them that if they met with the dean of students and presented this information, they would get the changes they were seeking.

They confessed to me that in lieu of extended visitation hours they and their friends were using underground tunnels to meet up with students of the opposite sex. I was shocked! This is why some of these old-fashioned rules need to change with the changing times. You can't fight human nature. The better course is to show students how to do things the right way—and then get out of their way.

I'm not naive. I understand college students will want to be intimate with one another. The girls were not supposed to have sex in the dorms at Mundelein, but obviously we couldn't monitor what was happening behind closed doors—and didn't want to. I recognize that times change and we have to change with them, but my personal views on this subject have not changed over the years. I believe it is immoral for people to have premarital sex.

One of the reasons I am concerned about young people having sex before marriage is because it can lead to unexpected pregnancies. Needless to say, I also believe abortions are immoral, although I think this matter should be left out of politics completely. That just messes things up. People in religious life handle these matters better than politicians. I'd rather have churches, doctors, and ethicists be involved in these conversations than lawmakers.

I understand that when young people are in love, they want to share that love physically, but I maintain that the proper thing is to wait until you are married. Does all this make me old-fashioned? I suppose so. I guess I'll have to stay that way. I'm more than a hundred years old, you know.

My move back to Chicago in 1961 made it more difficult for me to see my family, but I still traveled out to California a couple of times a year to visit. I loved visiting my brothers and their families, and it was always a delight to see my nieces and nephews. I had plenty of aunts and uncles who were happy to dote on me. And my parents were still full of energy and love. Each time I left, I felt a pang of sadness saying goodbye, but I was also reminded how incredibly blessed I was to be raised among people who loved me so much.

On New Year's Eve in 1967, my brother Ray, his wife, and their five children went to visit my parents. My mother had a bad cold, but she insisted to my father that she was going to clean the house. My dad ran an errand to the bank, and when he came home, he found her lying on the kitchen floor. She had had a massive stroke.

When I got word of what happened, I immediately made

arrangements to go see her. Mom was in the hospital, and though she was in very bad shape, she had some cognitive awareness of who was around her. My dad told her that I would be there soon because I was coming to San Francisco on a business trip. He didn't want her to know how bad things were. I tried to arrive in time to see her, but God had other plans. She died while I was on the plane. She was seventy-four years old.

My brothers met me at the airport and delivered the sad news. They had trouble finding me at first because they had forgotten I was no longer wearing a habit. It had been quite some time since they had seen me in contemporary clothes. They thought I had missed the plane and were about to go to lunch when they spotted me in the terminal. We had a good laugh about that, which we needed. Laughter really is the best medicine.

We drove to my parents' house and made the arrangements to bury my mother. I spent a week with Dad as we grieved together. He asked if I could take her clothes. He felt it would make things more difficult for him if her clothes were still in the house, and he wanted them to go to people who needed them. I knew a lot of sisters who were very much in need of new clothes, so I brought some back to Chicago.

My brothers lived in Marin County, so they were able to keep a close eye on our dad. Eventually he moved out of Napa Valley to be closer to them. It was a very, very difficult time. It's always toughest around the holidays, when we had so many memories. A year after Mom died, he said to me, "I can finally talk about your mother without crying. It doesn't mean I love her any less. It just means that God is taking care of me."

Sometimes people think that having faith means never being

angry, hurt, or sad. That's not true at all. Separation from anybody you love is difficult. We can trust God's plan, believe that our loved ones who have left us have gone to heaven, and still mourn their passing. Sadness and suffering are a part of life. If you have faith, those things can bring you closer to God. I believe it's God's purpose to help us through the suffering, not avoid it altogether.

I felt my mother's loss deeply, but I did not get angry at God. I was glad she was no longer suffering and that she did not have to live in a compromised state as a result of the stroke. My mom was an independent woman, and that would have embarrassed her. It would have been a huge burden on my father as well. I prayed often and trusted that God has a reason for everything. The time will come for all of us to be called home.

Times of loss, sadness, and tragedy really test our faith. I once knew a married couple whose newborn baby died when he was only one day old. That is not the type of thing that people ever get over. They just learn to live with the pain. It took a long time for those parents to reconcile what happened with their belief and trust in God. We had a person at Mundelein who taught a course on death and dying, and he was helpful to them. When they had another child, he cautioned them to make sure they treated their living child as an individual and not think of him as a replacement for the one they lost. I had several conversations with the parents as well. What can you say? Nothing will ease that kind of pain, although time helps soften its edges a bit. When they expressed their frustrations that God would allow this to happen, I told them, "It's okay to get mad at God. You can talk to Him any way you want."

I gave the same advice to a young woman who was about to get married but was hurting because her father had died the year before and wouldn't be there to walk her down the aisle. I told her, "Go to church and tell God you're really mad at Him for allowing that."

Being mad at God is not the same thing as not believing in Him. You can't be mad at something that doesn't exist, right? I believe God expects us to have a relationship with Him, and that relationship has many different dimensions. Like all relationships, it goes through ups and downs, and it matures over time. God made us fully human. We're all sinners. We're all flawed. He tests our faith for a reason. Getting mad at God is a way of expressing—and keeping—our faith.

Losing my mom when we did was a shock to all of us. I love her deeply and miss her every day, but I know completely in my heart that she is with God in heaven, and that someday we will be reunited. In the meantime, down here on earth, I have a lot more work to do.

Nine

Loyola

If you keep moving, eventually
you'll find your balance.

DURING MY TENURE AT Mundelein, I taught most every subject and held most every job—or so it seemed. I taught methods classes in the education department, supervised student teachers, and conducted a reading clinic for children in the neighboring schools. I served as director of Summer Session, freshman dean, sophomore dean, assistant dean, director of Weekend College, director of the Mundelein College Reading Clinic, and even acting dean. (Today they call that an *interim* dean, although when I had the job I surely had to act like the real thing!) I also remained the director of student employment and head resident of Coffey Hall.

I held plenty of positions outside the university as well. I was a member of the Chicago Area Reading Association, the National Academic Advising Association, and the National Council for Accreditation of Teacher Education, as well as an academic governing association in the Midwest. I traveled to meetings all over the country. We had BVM senates in those days as well, and for six years I ran the logistics and hospitality. I didn't seek out any of these positions. They all found me. I had hardly any downtime, but I slept well.

This was not uncommon for those of us who worked at Mundelein. We all wore many hats, and on a whim, we could be handed a whole new set of responsibilities. We might not have had any experience or expertise in that area, but it didn't matter. The job was ours, and we had to learn on the fly.

So I adapted. If I didn't know something, I asked questions. Too many people are afraid to use those three magic words: "I don't know." Why is that? We can't possibly know everything, and if we pretend that we know more than we do, it usually leads to bigger problems. One of the few times I asked to get out of an assignment was when they offered me a position that oversaw the financial assistance process. That is a position that requires a high level of expertise, as well as a great deal of time, because you have to keep up with all the changing regulations. My fear was that if I messed up, it would cost a student a chance to earn greatly needed scholarship money. I didn't want a young person's education to be threatened by my lack of knowledge.

Whenever Sister Ann Ida asked me to assume a new responsibility, she gave me time to pray and discern whether it was something I would be able to do. I wanted to do what was best for Mundelein and for me. Sometimes I would get out a notebook and list the pros and cons of my decision. I'm a big believer in writing. I hope pens and notebooks never go completely out of style.

I believe that serving in these various capacities brought me closer to God and burgeoned my faith. It brought me joy and happiness to know I was helping young people advance their education. I especially loved working with freshmen because they changed so quickly. When those kids arrived on campus, bright-eyed and bushy-tailed, I warned the parents that they would be amazed at how much change they would see when their children came home for Christmas break.

As I floated from job to job, I can't say I had a master plan in mind. I wasn't trying to climb a ladder; I didn't aspire to sit in the president's office one day. I've never had that kind of ambition. I was just going with the flow. If I had ever been asked to fulfill a president's job, I would have stepped in and done the best I could, but to be honest I think I'm a good second person. Not working in the very top jobs saved me a lot of grief over the years.

I pride myself on being the ultimate team player. Wherever I worked, it was my primary ambition to see the school succeed, and I was happy to play whatever role I could in making that happen. Although I don't strive for the top position, I do value ambition. It's great to dream big and pursue those dreams with vigor. But like so many things in life, we must practice moderation. If we don't, ambition can warp our perspective. Some people might think it's in their blood that they must have a certain job, but then when they don't get it, it's tough on everybody who lives with them. Or if they do get it and the results aren't as expected, they feel lost. Be careful what you wish for, as the saying goes.

Ambition is a healthy driver, but we need not allow it to make us lose our sense of ourselves. One trap that I think many people fall into is that they chase money too much. I believe it's more important to derive purpose from your work than to make a lot of money. Besides, if you really love your job, you'll work hard at it and get good at it, and eventually someone will pay you well for it.

I've seen many of my fellow teachers change schools for a "bigger" job that paid more, only to regret that they left a good situation. Whenever I hear others say they don't like their job or the professional path they have chosen, I encourage them to make a change. We spend so much time at our jobs, it's important that we feel good about being there. Life is too short to be unhappy.

My niece Jeanne, who was my brother Raymond's oldest daughter, came to Mundelein as a freshman in 1973. She moved into my residence hall, which was not an easy situation for her. She got teased quite a bit, and I offered encouragement by reminding her how wonderful she was and that she shouldn't let wisecracks from other people get to her. A few years later, her sister Janet transferred from California State University to Mundelein. We became extremely close during their time at Mundelein, and we remain close to this day.

Any connection I could maintain to my family was special to me. I was approaching an age when some of my aunts and uncles were passing away. But my father was still alive and remained independent for a long time. He lived in his own apartment, did his own cooking and driving, played golf, and went on cruises with my brothers and their families. He was good friends with his neighbors. He never dated or found another woman, however, and never came close to getting married again.

For a couple of years after my mom died, he went to mass every day. Eventually he scaled back to once or twice a week. I'm sure there were times when he missed her terribly, but he rarely showed it. I thought it was remarkable when he was able to talk about our mother so freely. We didn't think he would ever get over losing her. Actually, "get over" isn't the right phrase. You never really get over that kind of loss, but hopefully at a certain point you are able to manage the pain. Trusting God helps immensely.

When my dad reached his early nineties, he started to slip mentally. He was having transient ischemic attacks (TIAs), which create temporary stroke-like symptoms, and although they don't typically cause permanent damage, they put a lot of stress on the brain. While he was driving to church one morning, he lost control of his car and ran into a light post. A policeman came to assist him and brought him home. I visited that summer for a couple of weeks, and my brothers and I agreed we needed to have a difficult conversation with our father.

My brother arranged the visit, and together we discussed the future. My brother said, "Dad, I'm not the type of person to beat around the bush. We would like to talk to you about your future." We went through all the options. We discussed the possibility of his living with one of my brothers, but Dad didn't want to be a burden. He actually made the suggestion to move into Nazareth House, an assisted living facility a few blocks from my brother's house. It was a popular place, and there was normally a long waiting list; however, at the time, they had very few men, which offered my dad a faster entry, and he was given a room shortly thereafter.

He was ninety-five years old when he died on Ash Wednesday in 1990. Both my brothers were with him when he passed. Even though he was very old and we knew it was coming, it was still a painful loss for all of us. You never quite realize how much you depend on your parents until they're gone. No matter how old I got, when I was home, my father always treated me like I was sixteen. "I'm grown up now, Dad," I'd admonish him, but no matter. That's just how parents are. Once, when I mentioned to my brother that he must be relieved his children were grown up and moved out, he replied, "I worry about them just as much now as when they were kids."

I still miss my parents and think about them every day, but I like to think about how happy they must be together in heaven and how lucky I was to be their daughter. God has blessed me in so many ways, none bigger than the gift of my parents.

By the mid-1980s, Mundelein was coming under increasing financial duress. Our enrollment had been steadily declining each year, and there was no indication that the trend was going to reverse.

However, we received a small boost in the early 1980s with an influx of Muslim students. The Muslim population had been growing around Chicago. They typically went to Muslim schools, but one day a pair of fathers came to our campus and asked if their daughters could attend Mundelein. The fathers were concerned because Mundelein had extended the visitation hours in the residence halls to allow more opportunity for non-students, including boys, to socialize with the young ladies. These fathers were quite conservative and made it clear they did not want their daughters fraternizing with boys in their dormitories.

As assistant dean, I was involved in the conversations to help figure out a way around the problem. We had a dozen or so nuns who lived on the top floor of an apartment building that doubled as a hotel. The nuns were asked if they would be willing to allow two Muslims girls to live with them. They said of course. When we proposed this solution to the fathers, they were delighted. They assured us that if their daughters had a good experience at Mundelein, there would be many more Muslim girls who would want to apply. And that's exactly what happened.

Though the boost helped, it wasn't enough. By the late 1980s, we were barely surviving. There just were not enough young women who were interested in going to an all-female college anymore. We all recognized that unless drastic measures were taken, in a few years we would have to fold our tents. Fortunately for us, a solution emerged: an official affiliation with Loyola, our brothers next door.

We had enjoyed a great relationship with Loyola for a long time, having shared campuses, professors, and other resources, so it was natural for us to explore that path. Loyola is run by members of the Society of Jesus, or Jesuits, a Catholic order that was founded by Ignatius of Loyola and six of his students in Paris during the early sixteenth century. The Jesuits and the BVM community have long had a close relationship. When the BVM sisters opened their motherhouse in Iowa, they received tremendous support from a local order of Jesuits. Many of the retreats the BVM sisters attended in those early days were directed by the Jesuits.

It's not surprising the two communities have always clicked, because we share similar philosophies. The Jesuits practice what is known as "liberation theology," which emphasizes the liberation of the poor and the oppressed. Their stated mission is to help people "find God in all things." They have always encouraged tolerance for other religions and supported the idea that everyone should get an education.

For several months, our board of trustees engaged in conversations with Loyola about setting up a formal affiliation. As the conversations became more serious, a swath of our alumni objected to the idea. We listened to their perspectives and opinions, but I also noticed that most of them were not sending their own daughters to Mundelein. Like many young people, their daughters wanted to attend coed schools.

After many conversations and lots of careful planning, in the spring of 1991 we made it official. This move has been characterized as a "merger," but technically it was an affiliation. Under the new arrangement, Mundelein would cease to exist under its own name and would instead become part of Loyola University.

This was not an easy transition for any of us. Our president, Carolyn Farrell, did her best to protect our legacy. She helped establish the Gannon Center for Women and Leadership at Loyola, named in honor of Sister Ann Ida Gannon. Mundelein's archives are kept in the Gannon Center. She carried over many parts of our curriculum, such as our Peace Studies program and the Weekend College program. It wasn't the same as preserving Mundelein altogether, but it was a whole lot better than going out of business.

Sister Carolyn worked closely with Loyola's president, Father Baumhart, and they had a productive relationship. I wasn't sure if I was going to be able to stay there or be sent to another school.

Everyone met with human resources to help map out a plan. Fortunately, we were able to keep most of our faculty on staff, and in much the same roles. That included our kitchen and cleaning staff as well.

It was a challenging time, because change—especially massive change—makes people nervous. It makes us feel insecure. There were so many small changes inside this big change that it was difficult to wrap my head around it. I've learned that the more personal things become to us, the harder it is to see them change. We might feel as though in the new paradigm, we won't be accepted—and everybody wants to be accepted. No matter what kind of leader we think we might be or how much positive work we've done in our positions, when we're trying to step into somebody else's shoes, or wear our own shoes a different way, our steps will be unsteady at first. But if we keep moving, eventually we'll find our balance. The key is to keep our faith, both in ourselves and in God, until that happens.

It was tricky because in order for the affiliation to work, each university had to sacrifice something for the greater good. People may say this is something they are willing to do, but often when it comes time to make the move, they become reluctant. It was particularly inconvenient for people who had to move into different living spaces because we were repurposing many of the buildings. Some sisters moved into off-campus apartments, and Loyola helped cover their expenses. The president at Loyola asked me to help in managing this transition, although, for a time, we had to work in secret because we knew a lot of people wouldn't be happy about it. It's good to solicit people's opinions, but in the end, you have to have one person making a final decision. Otherwise you'll be debating for so long that nothing ever gets done. You can't make everybody happy.

After we met with human resources, we were assigned to new positions, although for the most part they tried to keep us in similar roles. I continued my work at the Weekend College, which was incredibly important to me. I worked out of a separate office downtown on weekends. I also continued as an academic advisor, which allowed me to make sure the students were properly on track to graduate.

A good portion of our student body said they felt betrayed. However, over time, I believe most of them saw why this was the best course for our school. Among the many benefits Mundelein enjoyed was a multimillion-dollar upgrade to our main building, which had become quite out of date. It's a first-class building now, and it would never have been renovated if we had not affiliated with Loyola.

Some of our faculty never truly bought into the affiliation. I respected their positions, but I felt that in the end, they were only hurting themselves. I may have had questions at the outset, but once the deal went through, I felt that the best course was to embrace the new arrangement, make the most of it, and influence the decision makers any way I could.

Once we affiliated, I was assigned the title of assistant dean, and I served as a freshman and sophomore academic advisor. Eventually I became an assistant vice president and academic vice president. I was also invited to take part in the RCIA program, which stands for Rite of Christian Initiation of Adults. That was a program for people who wanted to enter the Catholic faith. Some of them were marrying a Catholic; others were born Catholic but hadn't received the sacraments.

Working with adults was a terrific complement to my work with students, but I never wanted it to be a replacement.

I helped run another program for Traditional Age Freshmen (TAF). These were students who were not quite ready to take a full course load. We invited fifty of them to come in and take eleven hours as part-time students. My codirector and I met with two dozen students individually each week, and we assembled a booklet for the curriculum. We used the ACT test to demonstrate the progress we were making with these students. It was an innovative program, so much so that we were invited to Detroit to present our methods and findings to an educators' conference.

One Sunday morning during the winter of 1992, I fell and broke my hip while walking to work. They called for an ambulance, and I was in a great deal of pain. I underwent surgery, during which the doctors inserted titanium to make the hip stronger. I tried to get people to call me the Bionic Nun after that, but it never caught on.

I always felt young and spry, but let's face it, the years were adding up. In August 1994, I turned seventy-five years old. I thought I would keep working until I couldn't walk anymore, but then Loyola came to me with a generous retirement package. It covered expenses that would support me for a long time, plus health insurance. In fact, I would actually earn more money as a retiree than I was making as a salaried employee, although of course anything I earned went directly to the BVM community. Even with this package, I was able to keep working, with the caveat that I could only put in five hundred hours a year, although I could volunteer as much as I wanted.

I am not exactly the kind of gal who sails gently into the sunset. I stayed quite active, and it wasn't long before I was reenlisted. Shortly after I "retired," Father Piderit, Loyola's president, mentioned that some members of the men's and women's basketball teams were falling behind academically. He wondered if I might be able to help. He wasn't asking me to serve as the official academic advisor, just to give them study tips and guide them through the material. So that's what I did.

I referred to myself as "the Booster Shooter," because it was my job to boost their grades. Motivation wasn't a problem because the players all knew that in order to stay eligible to play, they had to maintain at least a C average. After a couple of years, their academics improved so much that they didn't need me anymore.

Being the Booster Shooter didn't take up much time, so I also volunteered to be a desk worker in the professional building at Saint Joseph Hospital. I had already begun to work in a doctor's office, and then her husband, also a doctor, asked me to work for him. He hired me to help him organize his office three days a week. I ended up working for him for eleven years.

Sometimes when people retire they become reclusive. I could never have just sat in my room or been by myself all the time. I would have missed people too much—especially young people. I needed to wake up with purpose every day. I didn't have any desire to move to a place with warm weather like a lot of senior citizens do. I had lived in Chicago for thirty years, and it was home now. The cold stopped bothering me long ago, and I was comfortable there and liked what I was doing.

I figured I would just keep moving along this path and help out wherever I could, with a big smile but minimal fanfare. Little did I know that things were about to change. A new assignment was heading my way, and though it would take a few years, it turned out to be the most transformational and transcendent position of my life.

Ten

Jumping into Hoops

Life is a team sport.

IN THE FALL OF 1994, Father Piderit casually mentioned to me that the men's basketball team was in need of a new chaplain. He wondered if I might be interested. I don't think he realized what a big sports fan I was, but by then I was going to all the games anyway. I loved watching those kids play and the energy they brought to campus. And my role as the Booster Shooter had allowed me to get to know many of the coaches and players personally. I told Father Piderit I'd give it a shot.

To be honest, I wasn't quite sure what a team chaplain did. There were no notes or instructions left over from those who had done it in the past. So I did what I always did when I got a new job—dove in with full enthusiasm and good intentions and trusted that whatever I didn't know, I'd come to know in due time.

By that time, Loyola basketball's success in the early 1960s was very much a relic of the past. The Ramblers had been to only one NCAA tournament since 1968 and none in the previous ten years. We had just brought in a new coach, Ken Burmeister, a former assistant at DePaul who had been hired after the school fired the previous coach for going 1–9 in our conference. Ken was one tough cookie. I watched him run practice, and he really drove the boys hard. It seemed to me that they were responding to his methods, but because the program had been down for so long, we just didn't have much talent at first.

Ken's first season was a real struggle, to put it mildly. The team only won five games all season and went 2–13 in our league, the Midwestern Collegiate Conference. It wasn't easy for Ken to keep the players' spirits up, but I thought he did an excellent good job under the circumstances. Our home arena, Alumni Gym, held approximately two thousand people, the equivalent to a large high school gym. If people arrived early enough, they could sit wherever they wanted.

I don't know how other schools do it, but at Loyola we are serious about academics. On the first day of class, each player provides a letter to all of his teachers, listing the days he will miss class. There are some people in academia who believe athletes should never miss class, but that's not realistic. That's why all the teams have academic advisors, so they can ensure the players are able to make up the work. Playing on a sports team is a great commitment, and the athletes need all the help they can get.

I've never believed that colleges should limit an athlete's coursework. Just like any other student, college athletes have to develop time management skills and make decisions for themselves as to what they can handle. A college student's academic work can determine their professional path, especially if that person wants to continue on to graduate school. After all, the vast majority of college athletes won't end up playing professional sports. As a university, we need to make sure athletes are fully educated while trying to win games. If they're not, that's on us, not them.

———

Like all coaches, one of Ken's biggest challenges was understanding that every player has a different perspective and set of experiences, and so each player is motivated in his own way. That's why empathy is so important in a leader. It's easy to say, "Oh, these kids are old enough to understand," but many times they don't fully understand everything that is happening in their lives.

I remember one basketball player who was nervous about going home for the holidays because his parents had just gotten divorced, and he didn't know where he should stay. He confided this to me and told me he was considering staying with friends so he wouldn't have to choose between his parents. He was also considering staying in Chicago. I didn't have any easy answers for him. I just listened, mostly. But I did encourage him to go home and figure a way to be with his family. When he returned to campus, he told me he was glad that he had followed my advice.

In 1996, we moved into a new home court, Gentile Arena, a brand-new facility that was more than twice the size of Alumni Gym. We still struggled to win games those first few years, but we had a skilled three-point shooter named Derek Molis who transferred from Fordham. There was a group of elementary school kids who used to sit on the balcony above the court. Every time Derek made a three-pointer, they hung a sign with the number "3" on it. One time he made eight in a game, and it really brought down the house. Derek also had a nice disposition even though he'd experienced loss. His mother died when he was a senior in high school, but his dad encouraged him to play for Loyola. Derek went on to own a sporting goods store in suburban Chicago.

The one thing I really look for when I watch the games is who is a team player. In sports, it's not just about excelling as an individual or scoring the most points. You have to match your skills with the rest of the team's and be willing to do whatever it takes to win. I've seen many occasions, both on our team and among our opponents, where a player might score a lot of points, but then his teammates are standing around watching instead of contributing. That can work in the short term, but in the long term those teams have a difficult time succeeding. This is a major reason why I believe in the power of athletics to teach important skills those players can use forever. Life is a team sport, after all.

Matt Hawes, who played forward from 1992 to 1996, was a great example of a team player. Another one of my favorites from those years was Javan Goodman, who was recently inducted into our athletics Hall of Fame. Javan played with great flair. You never saw anybody jump so high! And he was such a nice young man, very humble.

Dominic Okon was a quiet player but very effective. He later became an assistant coach for us, and then he took an assistant's job at Wichita State. I'm sure he'll make an excellent head coach someday, although when Wichita State came to play us, I had to explain to him before the game that I was sorry to have to root against his team. He understood, of course.

The bulk of the public's attention goes to the players who get the most minutes, but some of my favorites over the years barely got into the games. We had a player named Brad Tice who was on the bench most of the time, but he was so enthusiastic and supportive, the other players called him the "bench clown." Brad kept everybody involved in the game whether they were on the court or not. He later became a primary school teacher, which didn't surprise me in the least.

Later on we had a player named Justin Coons who almost never got off the bench. During the final minutes of the game, the fans would chant, "We want Justin!" If he got in and made a basket, it would bring down the house. He was a wonderful young man and joined the Marine Corps after he graduated.

Unfortunately, as our coach, Ken didn't meet the expectations placed on him, so in 1998, Loyola replaced him with Larry Farmer, who had once been a very good player at UCLA. Larry had actually spent three years as UCLA's head coach, but that was a difficult job because the fans always expected their coaches to win as much as John Wooden had.

Larry had two young kids, and his wife brought them to all Loyola's games. He was incredibly gracious about letting me be around the team as much as possible. I even rode the bus for away games. I learned early on that Larry preferred his buses to be quiet. During the ride to a game, I was chatting a little too loudly in the back of the bus, and Larry said to me nicely but firmly, "Sister Jean, we don't talk on the bus. We concentrate." I zipped my lips real fast! He never had to say that to me again.

The team only won nine games in Larry's first season. The next year he brought in a talented freshman guard named David Bailey. David was only five foot eight, but he never let his size stop him from competing. His brother played for the University of Illinois Chicago, which was in our league. Whenever we played UIC, their mother would come to the games wearing a T-shirt that was half Loyola and half UIC. She was careful not to show any preference.

One of the amazing things about following a team so closely is you get to watch these young men progress from year to year. There was a forward on the 2000 team named Corey Minnifield who didn't play much at first, but then he got better every season and ended up in the starting lineup. I was so proud of him. We only see the results during the games, but that kind of progress happens because someone is putting in a lot of practice hours and especially in the off-season. Sometimes we expect too much from these guys. We forget how young they are and how big of a jump it is to go from high school to college. I know that is an especially big challenge for players who receive a lot of publicity when they are in high school. They are written about and highly ranked, and then they come in as freshmen and think they should be star players right away.

I get a kick when I see our former players come back to the games with their wives and children. I look at those kids and ask their dads, "Are you going to send them to Loyola?" You can never start recruiting them too early, you know.

The 2001 team marked the arrival of a pair of freshmen, Anthony and Antoine Smith, who were identical twins. It was challenging to tell them apart. Their mother lived in St. Louis and came to every home game. Sadly, Anthony was diagnosed with leukemia shortly before he graduated in 2005. He went through chemotherapy and was in remission, but he later died a day before his twenty-fifth birthday. Several of Anthony's former teammates traveled to St. Louis for his funeral. It was a huge loss for our Loyola family.

⸻

I was working the reception desk at the medical center on the terrible morning of September 11, 2001. When I heard about the terrorist attacks in New York, I immediately informed all the doctors. The news kept worsened throughout the day. When my shift ended, I headed to my office at the downtown campus to be with the students. Some of them had friends and relatives in New York, and it took some time for them to find out whether they were safe. The schools had counselors on hand to speak with students who were especially upset. Mostly, all of us just shared the shock and grief together. It was one of those moments when you don't really know what to say. You just pray as hard as you can.

That fall, Loyola started the academic year under our new president, Father Michael Garanzini. The university was in bad shape when he took over. The facilities had become outdated, and enrollment was an annual challenge. Father Garanzini knew he had a lot of work to do, so he came in with a lot of energy. He understood that feathers would be ruffled, but that was okay with him. All leaders have to navigate resistance if they want to make change.

Father Garanzini's arrival coincided with an effort by the BVM community to bring many older, retired sisters back to Dubuque to live out their days at the motherhouse. They had put a lot of money into renovating the place, and plenty of sisters were happy to make the move. I wasn't seriously considering it, but Father Garanzini did not want to lose me, which flattered me. He embarked on what he referred to as a conspiracy to sweeten my deal, and I stayed. We became fast friends after that.

One of the reasons Father Garanzini wanted to keep me around was that I had been there so long and therefore could help him make his case to the younger sisters who might be skeptical of changes he wanted to make. Both of us lived on the main campus but often worked at Loyola's Water Tower Campus downtown. We rode the bus together, and he would pepper me with questions about what I was hearing around the school. He knew I had my ear to the ground, and he wanted to squelch any problems before they grew too large.

I especially appreciated Father Garanzini's approach toward education. He frequently told us, "Get out of the students' way. Let them be." Sometimes that's the best advice, for teachers as well as parents. It's our job to encourage young people to pursue their dreams—and then give them the space to work through their own challenges instead of trying to fix everything for them all the time.

Father Garanzini saw that our athletic facilities were way behind the times, but he put a higher priority on sprucing up the academic buildings and residence halls, and then making sure the faculty were well paid. He launched a five-year, $100 million capital campaign and appointed me as cochair of the Reimagine Program. The purpose was to encourage people to buy into his vision of what the campus could look like.

Serving as cochair of that program was one of the most important jobs I've ever had. My cochair and I arranged for a variety of committees to meet with faculty and students so everyone could see the plans that were being put together. There were so many good ideas that came out of those conversations. For example, the students advocated for a climbing wall in the student center. I had never heard of such a thing, but we accommodated their request, and it became a popular feature. As cochair, I was given a monthly progress report, and then I wrote letters to all the committee folks and trustees to make sure they were apprised of what was happening.

Thanks to Father Garanzini, I continued to pick up all sorts of random jobs. At one point he asked me to supervise the bus stop at the Water Tower Campus. It was a somewhat chaotic situation because we had so many students using the bus to commute to our Lake Shore Campus, and they were overrunning the sidewalks. One day I asked the kids to move to the side, and a star volleyball player decided to challenge my authority. Standing at six foot nine, he looked down at me, grinned, and said, "Sister Jean, what if I don't feel like doing that today?"

I wrinkled my nose and replied, "Oh, I had two younger brothers. I know exactly how to handle you." He got into line.

Father Garanzini had a way of giving commands that sounded like suggestions. One day he said to me, "Sister Jean, I'm thinking we should start a program to get our students interacting with residents at The Clare. Don't you think that would be nice?"

I agreed, so I called an administrator at The Clare and asked for an appointment. It was a productive meeting as I discussed forming a group of students at Loyola and arranging regular visits to The Clare. The administrator loved the idea. "What is the program called?" he asked. I hadn't thought about a name yet, so I said I'd have to think about it. Eventually I decided to call it SMILE:

Students Moving into the Lives of the Elderly. That was the name for a similar program used at Loyola University in New Orleans.

I wanted the program to be relatively small and unstructured. Students weren't required to spend a specific number of hours, but they were asked to have a consistent presence at The Clare. We had about fifteen students participate in SMILE. The students visited with the residents, and oftentimes they helped them with their computers or telephones or grocery shopping.

SMILE turned out to be a wonderful program. You'd think those young people would be so different from the elderly folks they were caring for, but it didn't take long for all those differences to melt away. Many of the residents were retired lawyers, teachers, and professionals who remembered very well what it was like to be a college student. They related to the youngsters a lot better than you might think.

The main purpose of the SMILE program was to benefit the elderly residents, but the reason I loved it so much was because of what it did for the students. Many of them had grandparents, and I know they saw their loved ones in those residents. The program taught them to be patient because some of the elderly were sick, even though they weren't grumbling about it. They were taught that suffering is something that often comes with old age, and so people need to adjust to what is happening to their bodies and minds. Most of all, they learned firsthand the power of love. When we care for someone in need and show empathy toward that person, it strengthens them, and in turn it strengthens us too.

The COVID-19 pandemic put the SMILE program on hiatus, but I am hopeful it will resume once the pandemic has subsided. I've seen many beautiful friendships form out of the SMILE program over the years, and they didn't necessarily end when the students graduated. I know one fellow in particular who went on to get his master's degree at the University of South Florida. Whenever he came back to Chicago, he made a point to visit his friend at The Clare. That's a win if ever there was one.

Eleven

Worship, Work, Win

So long as there's a winner and a
loser, I'd much rather win.

UNFORTUNATELY, LARRY FARMER WAS not able to get the Ramblers to meet the expectations either. In 2004, the school decided it needed to make yet another change. It's never easy for me to see that happen because I form a relationship with the coaches and their families. It's especially hard on the players because they came to school expecting to play four years for the same coach. But everyone understands that while winning isn't the only thing that matters, it does matter quite a bit. If you don't win enough as a coach, you don't get to stick around.

Larry was replaced by Jim Whitesell. I was a little surprised by this appointment because Jim had never coached in Division I before. His previous job was at Lewis University, a Division II school in Romeoville, Illinois. But Jim achieved a lot of success there, and I was hoping he could do the same for Loyola.

Jim had a laid-back personality. He was very social and loved to tell stories. Once he stepped into a gym, however, he underwent a transformation. He believed he needed to change the culture inside the program, so during his first summer on campus, he scheduled the players to wake at 6 a.m. for intense workouts, followed by a team breakfast. The players weren't sure if they were on a basketball team or in the military, but it had its intended effect. In Jim's first season, we went 13–17 and 8–8 in the Horizon League. (That was the new name of our conference. The folks who ran it thought it would stand out more than the previous name, Midwestern Collegiate Conference.) The following year we went 8–8 in the Horizon again and won nineteen games, which was our highest total in twenty-one years. Gentile Arena was showing signs of life thanks to the new student section Jim created called the "Rambler Rowdies." We were two games from returning to the NCAA tournament in 2006, but we lost, 80–66, in the Horizon League tournament semifinals to Milwaukee.

With most of the team returning for the 2006–2007 season, we had high hopes. Some people picked us to win the league. During the tip-off luncheon that fall, I offered a prayer and asked God to help the Ramblers make the NCAA tournament. When Jim took the microphone, he thanked me and quipped, "I'm under enough pressure. I don't need more of it from God."

Regrettably, my particular prayer went unanswered. We finished third in the league and lost in the semifinals of the conference tournament, although we did win twenty-one games.

I was now into my second decade as team chaplain, and I was

making the role my own. I always prayed with the team before each game, but a gentleman who helped raise money for the athletic department one day asked, "Sister Jean, why don't you pray with the fans before the games?" I told him it was because nobody had asked me, but I didn't need to be asked twice. So at the next game, I walked onto the court in front of the scorer's table, took the microphone, and led the fans in a prayer. It was amazing to hear an arena that was so loud and boisterous grow quiet in an instant. People were excited about the game, but they were respectful of that moment. They especially liked it when I ended by saying, "Amen, and go Ramblers!"

I wasn't much for shooting, dribbling, and playing defense, but the players and coaches made me feel like a full member of the team. They even gave me a pair of maroon and gold Nikes. The words "Sister" and "Jean" were stitched on the heels, and I did my best to wear them out. I spent much of the night running around the arena, shaking hands, taking photos, and otherwise spreading good cheer. I emailed the players and coaches scouting reports on the upcoming opponents before each game, and after the game I wrote my thoughts about what I had seen. I wanted to be supportive, but I was also not afraid to critique or point out areas where I thought we were lacking.

I lived through all the ups and downs of the season, just like I was out there on that court. When those games were over, win or lose, I felt exalted and exhausted.

One day while having my picture taken on the court for a story that was being written about me for *Loyola* magazine, a few players happened to be walking by. The photographer asked them to join me. That photo ended up on the cover of the magazine. It was a fabulous picture because it really reflected the diversity of our program. Jim Whitesell had it enlarged and framed for me, and it hangs in my apartment to this day.

Those relationships with the players meant even more to me than the wins. I was constantly amazed at how they were able to balance their team responsibilities with their schoolwork. At one time we had four pre-med majors on the team. Some of them had applied to other schools, but they were told they couldn't be pre-med while also playing for the basketball team. I'm glad Loyola isn't like that. It's not easy to have a challenging course load while also being a high-level basketball player, but with enough determination it can be done.

Our twenty-one-win season turned out to be the best we ever did under Jim Whitesell. In the spring of 2011, following his fourth consecutive losing season in conference play, Jim was fired. That put us in the market for yet another head coach. It would be the fourth coach the team had since I had been named chaplain. I loved my Ramblers and my role inside the program, but we struggled to get out of this rut. It was all I could do to hold my anger at God. *Thank You, God, for all our blessings and the chance to serve You. But goodness gracious, can't we make March Madness just once?*

After many years of raising money and upgrading our academic buildings and dormitories, Father Garanzini finally turned his attention to athletics. With the help of Allan Norville, a wealthy alumnus, we started a capital campaign to build a fully dedicated practice facility. This was an especially important investment because it showed recruits we were serious about winning and that if they came to Loyola, they would always have a place to work out. Father Garanzini also hired a new athletic director, Grace Calhoun, who transferred from Indiana University.

Grace didn't take long to make her mark. Just a few months after she moved into her new position, she made the difficult decision to change basketball coaches. She worked quickly, and in early April, she announced the hiring of Porter Moser who had spent the previous four years as an assistant at Saint Louis University under Rick Majerus. I knew Majerus was well thought of, so that gave me confidence that Porter was prepared for this job.

Porter knew he was in for a tough rebuild, but his life experiences had readied him for the challenge. Porter's father was a successful businessman in the lumber industry in their hometown of Naperville, Illinois, but he insisted his kids understood the importance of hard work. When Porter was fifteen years old, he spent his summer working in his dad's lumberyard. When Porter reported for his first day, his dad told the other men, "Work him to the bone." And that's exactly what they did.

Whenever Porter's players ran into adversity, he talked to them about how to overcome because he had been through it himself. When Porter first went to Creighton as a freshman, he was so far behind the other players that the school didn't even give him a scholarship. He was a walk-on, presumably with very little chance of ever becoming a significant player there. Porter thought about transferring, but he decided to persevere. He finally got a chance to play as a sophomore and made the most of the opportunity. They put him on scholarship for his last two years. Porter's decision to continue at Creighton didn't just help his basketball career. It also led him to meet his wife, Megan.

The other major setback that Porter encountered was when he was fired as the head coach at Illinois State in 2007. The hardest part was breaking the news to his family. Porter wasn't sure he would ever get a chance to coach again, so when Majerus invited him a few weeks later to join his staff at Saint Louis, Porter jumped at the opportunity.

I met Porter at his introductory press conference. I'm not sure what he knew about me or what he expected, but I'm pretty sure he was surprised when he went to his office and found a stack of scouting reports on all our players that I had put together for him. I knew immediately that he was taking a personal interest in our guys. One of his first actions was invite the whole team to come to his house for a barbecue.

Porter came to Loyola having already developed resilience. He called it "competitive reinvention." It's funny how words can be so powerful. For example, sometimes when coaches show videos to their players, it can turn into an uncomfortable experience because the players are being criticized harshly. Porter referred to those videos as "Get Better Tapes." That way the players thought of watching them as a positive experience.

Given our history, the program didn't garner much fan support. The program had been down for so long that there wasn't much reason for people to attend games. That was especially true for the students, even though they didn't have to pay to get in. Porter recognized early on that this was a problem, and he sought to address it right away. He visited all the residence halls and pleaded with the students to come. He even brought lots of ice cream and handed it out on the condition that they would show up on game night. He convinced the administration to let him speak to all the incoming students during freshman orientation. He told them during these talks that they were an important part of the team. He even showed them how to properly distract opposing free throw shooters.

In 2013, at the start of Porter's second season, the team hosted a Midnight Madness celebration. That's when all the fans come out and watch the team hold its first practice. One of the highlights of the night was when our mascot, Lu Wolf, did a silly dance called "The Wobble" with the dance team. After the dance, the announcer introduced the team and the coaches, but when he called Porter's name, the coach was nowhere to be found. After waiting a few seconds to build suspense, Lu Wolf stepped forward, removed his head gear, and there was our head coach! Even the players didn't know it was Porter in that costume. Our fans may not have been convinced at that point that Porter was a good basketball coach, but there was no doubt that he knew how to boogie.

For all the energy Porter tried to bring, that first season was disastrous on the court. We won only seven games all season and went 1–17 in the Horizon League. But hey, nowhere to go but up, right?

The only thing Porter could do was continue to bring in guys who were not only good players but good people. The new recruits played hard and bought into his way of doing things. Many coaches around the country were starting to bring in a lot of transfers, but Porter's preference was to recruit players as freshmen and then work with them over time to develop their bodies and skills. That way our teams knew what to expect because they had been there awhile.

Things got easier for us in 2012 when Butler left the Horizon

League (they went to the Atlantic 10, and then after one season there, they moved into the Big East). Wichita State also moved to the American Athletic Conference in 2017, leaving the Missouri Valley Conference, which Loyola had joined in 2013. Those had been the two most dominant programs in our league. Their departure made the competition a little easier, but it also made it more difficult for our schools to make the NCAA Tournament. Basically, if we didn't win the conference tournament, we probably wouldn't be in March Madness. That really ratcheted up the pressure on everyone.

Although we didn't win a lot of games during Porter's first few seasons, his energy was infectious. There is a rule that says players are supposed to sit during games, but Porter wanted our guys up and cheering as much as possible. If the referee warned him that the bench needed to be sitting, Porter would pretend to chastise the reserves and then wink and smile at them to let them know he liked what they were doing. And there was always a guessing game with the fans as to how long Porter would keep his jacket on. It wouldn't take long after the tip that he removed it and tossed it aside. Some Loyola fans even started a @PortersJacket Twitter feed. At the end of every game, Porter went over to the student section and thanked them for coming. It didn't matter if there were twenty of them or two hundred, he was going to make sure they knew how much they were appreciated.

Regardless of what the final score was, all of us in the Loyola family understood what really mattered in life. That was never demonstrated better than on Senior Night in 2013. One of the players being honored was Jordan Hicks, a six-foot-six guard from Minnesota. He was a talented player, but his career never really got going because he was injured so much. Yet that wasn't the biggest challenge for him. When Jordan was a senior in high school, his mother, Carla, was diagnosed with breast cancer. It eventually spread into her lungs and her brain. She missed a lot of his games, but she was in Gentile Arena for Senior Night. It was very emotional when she came onto the court for the ceremony, but the real shock was when Jordan scored a career-high twenty-six points to help us beat Cleveland State. When the game ended, Jordan went over to his mom to give her a big hug, and then the entire team and coaching staff gave him a group embrace. Carla lived long enough to see her son graduate from college, and then she died the next day. May God bless her beautiful soul.

At the start of the 2013–2014 season, we made a huge change and joined the Missouri Valley Conference. Father Garanzini and our administration had been in discussions with the conference about joining them for a while. The other schools in the Valley were skeptical because we had been losing for so long and were way behind with our facilities. But they could see the progress we were making, and Father Garanzini convinced them we were serious about building a competitive program.

Porter proved him right. We went 4–14 in our first season in the Valley, but the next season we went 8–10. We also won twenty-four games overall, the most the Ramblers team had won in thirty years. Porter was turning the corner and building momentum.

Our leading scorer that year was Christian Thomas. I don't know that I've ever seen another player give so much effort, both physically and emotionally. Not only did he play hard, he wanted his teammates to play hard too. This took a big toll on Christian. There were plenty of times I thought he looked too tired to be out there, but I think he was afraid to admit that to Porter, because then Porter would take him out. Christian knew how to play physically and use his body without fouling.

As you can tell, basketball fascinates me. It's like a game of chess. The coaches keep substituting players to react to what the other coach is doing. It made me dizzy sometimes to see the way Porter shuffled his players in and out of the games. I took those scouting reports I sent to the players seriously. I did not want to give them any incorrect information that would hurt our chances. Thanks to the internet, I could look up what opposing players had done in previous games and then pass along helpful pointers.

During my pregame prayers, I tried to mix in some X's and O's along with my calls for divine intervention. "Good and gracious God, yes, we do want to win tonight, and we know that with Your help we can do it. But we understand that we must play as a team, play with our heads and our hearts, give our best every moment we are on the court. We plan to share the ball, direct it to the team member who is 'hot' tonight. We know that every shot from the charity line is important. If we can't make the perimeter points, we must work under the basket. Jeff, be careful of number 5. He looked good in warm-up time. Keep number 7 from the perimeter. Don't foul the best shooter on the team. We ask You, God, to help us play well, to avoid accidents, and to win. Amen."

Sometimes our team would go down in the dumps for no apparent reason. I've seen a player make so many shots one night that I thought he'd never miss again. Then the next night he can't make anything. When a player gets into a slump like that, he'll do anything to try to get himself out of it. I'll never forget the time when a guard named Milton Doyle, who had been shooting poorly for several games, asked if I would bless his hands. I said of course. Sure enough, he had a really good game that night. Before the next game, another player asked me to do the same thing. Pretty soon I was blessing everyone's hands. Did God really make their shots go in because I had blessed their hands? Maybe, maybe not. But they believed He had, which is the same thing as far as I'm concerned.

When word spread as to what I was doing, the referees started asking me to bless their hands too. I was happy to do so, but I also let them know that I prayed that they would call the game with equity. I now tease the referees that I think they need four of them on the court instead of three. It looks to me like they have trouble seeing the plays in the corners. I get very frustrated when I see them make a wrong call, especially if it goes against Loyola. I know this is another difficult part of being the coach. One time Porter got so mad about a bad call, he ran off the court and up a few stairs. Later on, a reporter asked him why he had done that. He replied, "I figured I'd go get a hot dog."

Serving as team chaplain was far from my only duty at Loyola. Here is a job description I wrote for myself in 2012: campus minister at WTC, supervisor of the shuttle-bus line, director of SMILE program, chaplain to the men's basketball team, assistant to the eucharistic ministers at the Sunday Liturgy in Madonna della Strada Chapel, director of prayer group in student resident hall, and member of the

Catholic Student Organization Book Club. Keep in mind this was eighteen years *after* I had retired.

When I spoke to various groups around campus, I was often referred to as "a friend to many." That was my main job title, and I loved it because I believe that all of God's children should be friends. We should have a great time together whether we are at a game; seeing one another in an elevator, at a formal meeting, at a meal; participating in Liturgy; or simply sharing prayer side by side. Friendship is enjoying the presence of God. God is everywhere, and so are my friends.

But I was quickly becoming most known for my work with the team. In 2011, I was informed that Loyola wanted to commission a bobblehead doll in my image. I thought they were pulling my leg. The next day they brought a drawing to my office to get my opinion— that's when I knew they weren't fooling. The one thing I noticed about the drawing was that there was no basketball. "What's that all about?" I said. So they fixed it by putting a ball in my hands. When the dolls came in, they promoted them to the public and promised to give one away to every fan who came to the next home game.

Two years later, a reporter from the *Chicago Tribune* noticed that this ninety-three-year-old nun in Nikes was going to all the games, holding prayers with the team before the game, and then leading the crowd in another prayer before the tip-off. She wrote a very nice article about me, which got me noticed even more at the games. I was also inducted into the Loyola athletics Hall of Fame. I'll bet there aren't many nuns out there who can say that.

I continued to go to sporting events all over campus. I liked to sit as close to the action as possible. When I went to softball games, I sat in the dugout. When I went to soccer games, I stood on the sideline. When I was at basketball games, I sat right near the court. However, all of that ended in 2014 when I was attending a volleyball game. I was sitting in my usual courtside seat when someone spiked the ball in my direction. I raised up my arm to keep it from hitting me, but it smacked me right in the face. I got two black eyes and a fractured wrist. They took me to the emergency room and everyone was so worried, but I was only mad that I had to miss the rest of the match. The person who hit me with the ball felt so terrible, but I assured him that I was doing fine.

From that point on, I was required to sit at a comfortable distance from the action. I acquiesced, but I didn't like it one bit.

As the school was making progress on our new practice facility, the Norville Center, Porter suggested we build a "wall of culture" in the weight room. He asked the players, coaches, and others around the athletic department to come up with words and phrases that would be painted on the walls. The idea was to inspire the guys while they were pumping iron. I was asked to contribute a phrase. Three words popped into my head: "Worship, work, win." I hadn't given it any thought before then, but those were the words that best reflected my philosophy on life and athletics.

Sometimes people catch me praying during the game and ask, "Were you praying for Loyola to win?" I tell them, "You better believe I was."

Winning is important because it gives the players the drive to work harder. The win is the payoff for all that effort. It's a wonderful, joyful feeling. As the saying goes, there's a reason they keep score. So long as there's a winner and a loser, I'd much rather win.

But we shouldn't lose sense of what's important just because we won—or lost, for that matter. I always appreciate how after our team wins, the players make sure to shake hands with the opponent and then circle around Gentile Arena thanking the fans for being there. It's very important for the fans to know that they're appreciated.

I am often asked, Is it appropriate to pray for the Ramblers to win? Of course it is! I believe God gives all of us talents, and it's up to us to use them as best we can. It's the same thing if we ask God to heal someone we love who is sick. We don't know if God will grant our wish, but I still think it's good to pray. You should do everything within the rules and standards of fair play to try to win the game, and if you don't win, you have to be a good sport about it. That is all God asks of us.

Does God really care who wins a basketball game? Maybe He cares more than we think. If nothing else, I imagine God must laugh sometimes when someone prays to win a game. God sees a lot of horrible stuff going on. Sometimes He needs a good laugh. I'd like to think I give Him a chuckle every time I say into that microphone, "Amen, and go Ramblers!"

Even though I lived two time zones away for so many decades, I managed to spend a good amount of time with my family in California. I went home every Christmas and spent a couple of weeks there every summer. I'm so blessed I was raised to appreciate the importance of doing things together as a family. My nephew Rich recently took his family on a big road trip across the country, which, to my delight, included a stop in Chicago. They visited a total of fourteen states and saw historical landmarks in each one, and then drove home on Route 66. The trip only lasted a few weeks, but the memories will last a lifetime.

Sometimes when I visited my brothers, we took a drive to Sausalito to visit the old family ark. The family sold it after all the kids had grown, but it still sits in the harbor, looking very much like a relic while offering a chance for fresh memories to its current owners. We had wonderful times on that ark.

My brother Ed was seventy-four when he died of lung cancer. He was a heavy smoker all his life. When we were growing up, just about everyone we knew smoked, including plenty of young people. My father was four years old the first time he tried a cigarette. One of his brothers got him to do it, and it made him so sick he thought he would never do it again. Although he took up the habit when he got older, when we started to learn about the damage that smoking caused, he quit. He tried to get Ed to quit as well, saying that going "cold turkey" was the only way to go. Unfortunately, Ed could never do it, and it ended up shortening his life.

My brother Ray was six years younger than me. When he finished high school, he found work painting houses. One day he came home from a job and told our dad that he had met the girl he was going to marry. When Dad asked who it was, Ray replied, "Margaret Hicks."

"Margaret Hicks?" my dad replied. "She's only twelve years old!"

"That's okay," Ray said. "I'll wait for her."

And that's exactly what happened. Ray joined the navy and fought in World War II. When he came home, Margaret was old enough to get married, and that's what they did. They were married for sixty-six years when Ray died of a heart attack in 2017 at the age of ninety. Unlike a lot of Catholics, Ray didn't want a wake. He didn't want people seeing him in that state. So we had a funeral mass, and as they wheeled Ray's casket out of the church, the organist played the song "Mack the Knife," just as Ray had requested. That's the kind of guy he was. That song made him feel happy, and he wanted people to feel that way at his funeral.

Naturally, I was sad when I lost my brothers. I was the oldest, and yet I'm the only one left. I talk to them and my parents all the time. I know they hear me in heaven.

Twelve

From Arch Madness to March Madness

The moment you let complacency set in, you're done.

LIFE CHANGED DRASTICALLY FOR me on November 17, 2017. I was leaving an appointment with my ophthalmologist at the medical building at Saint Joseph Hospital. As I stepped off the curb, I heard my hip crack. The pain was even worse than the sound. I collapsed to the ground. Fortunately for me, there was a woman nearby who rushed over to help. She called for an ambulance and put a jacket under my head. That woman was so kind, and I was so fortunate that such a good Samaritan had happened to be there when I fell.

When the paramedics arrived, they asked if I had hit my head. I assured them I hadn't. They took my vitals, which also looked okay.

I figured I would just go back inside Saint Joseph and get treated there, but the paramedic wanted me to go to a local trauma center. They drove me to Illinois Masonic Medical Center, where the next day I had surgery to repair my hip.

The discomfort was bad enough, but the accident also forced me to use a wheelchair. I really prized my independence, and now I was going to be beholden to someone pushing me around in a wheelchair. Because of that, I moved out of my room in Regis Hall and took an apartment at The Clare.

Worst of all, the accident happened at the start of basketball season. The last thing I wanted to do was miss any games. To that point, I had only missed two home games in my entire tenure as chaplain, but I had to miss a few while I recovered from the fall. I was very blessed that Tom Hitcho, who is a senior associate athletic director at Loyola, agreed to be my part-time caretaker. Tom was my primary wheelchair pusher, and he helped me get in and out of my Uber cars. I did most of my physical rehabilitation exercises at The Clare, helping that hip get stronger every day. One way or another, I was going to get back into Gentile Arena for home games.

This would be my twenty-third season as chaplain, and there was reason to think we would excel. Milton Doyle was the only senior who had graduated from the team that had an 18–14 record (8–10 Missouri Valley Conference) the previous season. Plus, I knew that Porter was bringing in talented freshmen. I had seen more than my fair share of losses over the years. I was ready to see wins.

The 2017–2018 season was going to be a big one for Loyola basketball. It was our one-hundredth anniversary season, and the school had plans to commemorate the centennial. Porter was now in his seventh season, and though I'm sure many schools would not have stuck by their coach for so long without making the NCAA tournament, everyone could see that he had the program moving in the right direction. The team he put together was experienced, talented, and filled with the type of character that Porter had set out to instill in the program from the moment he arrived.

The heart and soul of the roster was our three seniors. Donte Ingram was a six-foot-six guard from Chicago whom I had known since he was born. Donte's older brother, DaJuan Gouard, was part of our 2002 team that made it to the Horizon League tournament championship game. I remember Donte's parents bringing him to the games as an infant. They gave him earmuffs so he wouldn't be too disturbed by all the noise. Donte played for Simeon Career Academy, which is one of the most prestigious basketball schools in the country, and he could have played for a lot of colleges. He came to Loyola largely because of his family connection, and because of Milton Doyle, who was also from Chicago and had become great friends with Donte when he was playing on the high school circuit. That really shows the importance of treating every player well. If Milton had not complimented Porter, the program, and the university, Donte would not have come.

I was overjoyed when I heard Donte had committed to Loyola. You could tell right away that he played differently than his brother. He was a lot more aggressive, and he earned his minutes right at the start. He played a big role off the bench as a freshman, and during his sophomore season he became a starter. Donte's team-mates eagerly passed him the ball because he was a good scorer. You could see he enjoyed his time on the court. Basketball was never a chore for Donte. He would have played every minute of every game if Porter had let him.

Aundre Jackson was another senior. He was a six-foot-five for-ward who transferred in from junior college the year before. That's somewhat unusual for our program, but Aundre thrived both ath-letically and academically. He could dunk that ball! He had more dunks than anyone else on our team. It always got his teammates and the crowd excited.

Our other main senior was six-foot-three guard Ben Richardson. He was a skilled good three-point shooter, but he didn't take many shots because that would have detracted from the offense. Ben was also a great passer. Much like Milton helped to recruit Donte, Ben was instrumental in bringing in Clayton Custer, who after starting every game as a sophomore, Clayton was now a six-foot-one junior guard on the team. They had become best friends back in Kansas, so when Clayton decided to transfer after his freshman season at Iowa State, Ben did his best to convince him to consider Loyola. Porter was so excited about the possibility that as soon as Clayton reached out, he drove straight to Ames so he could take Clayton to lunch. Then he drove to Kansas City to meet with Clayton's par-ents. It wasn't Clayton's talent that attracted Porter so much as his attitude. He really believed Clayton could have a positive impact on our culture.

When I saw Ben and Clayton on the court together, I could tell they had known each other for a long time. That's when basket-ball is at its most beautiful, when players are working together so well that they don't even have to say anything. It's as if they know what the other is going to do before it happens.

Marques Townes was another tough and talented guard. He was a six-foot-four junior who was very much like Donte in that he played with his whole heart and gave it every ounce of strength when he was on the court. Sometimes when guys are out there, they're so intense and focused that you're not sure whether they're having a good time. That was never the case with Marques.

With the three seniors and two juniors returning, this was going to be one of Porter's most experienced teams. But we also had promising freshmen. One of them was Lucas Williamson, another guard from Chicago who was tough, speedy, and highly intelligent. I don't know what it is about our city, but Chicago seems to produce a lot of great guards like Isiah Thomas, Doc Rivers, and Derrick Rose. Lucas had played for another city powerhouse, Whitney M. Young Magnet High School, so he was not intimidated by coming to Loyola. Lucas's demeanor was so mature, I couldn't believe he was only a freshman. You never saw him lose his composure. When the team lost its way and started to come apart, Lucas was the first one to calm everyone down. Sometimes other players don't respond so well to that kind of thing, especially coming from a freshman, but our guys always respected Lucas.

The other freshman who came in ready to play right away was Cameron Krutwig who grew up in Algonquin, Illinois. He was a most unusual player. Cameron was a six-foot-nine center, but it seemed at times like he was more of a point guard. His teammates loved playing with him because he was such an excellent passer. When he first got here, I thought Cameron was kind of shy, but it didn't take long for him to come out of his shell. He was aggressive at driving to the basket and used his body to score inside and get fouled. Not only did that send him to the free throw line a lot, but it also put the opponents in foul trouble.

As the season got underway, I could see that we had a collection of real team players. You can tell who the coaches think are the team players because they're the ones who are on the floor at the end of the game. When I speak to the team and write my emails to the players, I always emphasize the importance of sharing the ball. I've watched enough basketball to know that teams struggle if they have really good pieces that don't fit well together. Our 2017–2018 team had great pieces that fit perfectly. They played hard, they played smart, and they liked and respected one another. That goes a long way when the game gets late and the score gets close.

Each day those players came into Gentile Arena, they passed by a wall that had the famous expression from Saint Ignatius of Loyola painted on it: "Go forth and set the world on fire." Little did any of us realize just how hot things were about to get.

The Ramblers got off to an 8–1 start that season, with the only loss coming at Boise State. That was our best record through nine games since the 1965–1966 season, and it gave us a lot of confidence heading into a big game at Florida on December 6. We were going to need that confidence because Florida was ranked No. 5 in the country, and Ben Richardson wouldn't be playing because he was still recovering from a hand injury he had suffered in our third game. Plus, the game was going to be in Florida's home arena. I couldn't make it to

Gainesville for the game, but I was locked on to my television screen back at The Clare, where everyone knew I was not to be disturbed until it was over.

The boys came in ready to play and before we knew it we were up by thirteen points. Florida stormed back in the second half, but we hung on for a 65–59 win. Everyone was thrilled, but Porter understood right away that sometimes winning a big game like that can hurt a team because everyone gets complacent. He acknowledged as much when he talked to reporters after the win. "Obviously, when you win a game like this, it's a good spotlight on you," he said. "But you want that spotlight to burn even more inside as we prepare and get better as the season goes on."

I can only imagine what the players were thinking. *Hey, Coach, we just beat the number five team in the country! Why are you acting so worried?* Well, it turned out that Porter knew what he was talking about. We came home and beat an overmatched Norfolk State team by twenty-eight points, but after that we lost three of our next four, including to Indiana State at home. Now we were 1–2 in the Missouri Valley Conference. This is another bad habit I've seen over the years, where a team plays up or down to the level of its competition. Our guys were getting up for the highly skilled teams like Florida, but they weren't as focused when they were playing teams that supposedly weren't so good—and it was costing them.

Part of the reason this is such a bad habit is that when you're winning, the other team wants to beat you. I know this because we were on the other side of it for so long. Many times when Loyola didn't have such a hot record, you could see the other teams weren't taking us seriously. That allowed us to win quite a few games we should not have won. If you want to be excellent at whatever you do, you have to be ready to compete every single time. The moment you let complacency set in, you're done.

One thing I always appreciated about Porter is that for all his frenetic energy, he had a great way of calming everyone down when they got too excited. If somebody made a mistake, Porter might take him out of the game, but he would tell him right away what he did wrong. He was equally intentional about pointing out when they did something right. Everybody needs a pat on the back once in a while. And some players need more pats than others.

Just like winning can be poisonous, losing can be good medicine. Those losses got everyone focused and believing what Porter had to say. As a result, the team buckled down and started to play much better. Their next game was on the road at Northern Iowa, which has always been one of the toughest teams in our conference. We won by six points. That was the start of a seven-game winning streak. We lost at Bradley by two points, and then we won another seven in a row. You could feel the excitement building around the campus, but part of me was holding my breath. I knew how hard the coaches and players were working. They deserved a real winning season, one that ended in the NCAA tournament.

Meanwhile, I was working just as hard with rehabbing my hip. This was no time to slack off! The wins piled up so quickly that we wrapped up the regular season championship of the Missouri Valley Conference before the regular season was even done. It was our first league title since 1985 and our first as a member of the Valley. When we completed our regular season with a 68–61 home win over Illinois State, our record stood at 25–5, and 15–3 in the conference.

That should have been enough to finally guarantee us a spot in March Madness, but unfortunately that is not how things work. Many conferences are able to get eight or nine teams into the tournament, but in a league like the Missouri Valley Conference, if a team doesn't win its conference tournament, it's challenging to get into that bracket. It took us two months to win that regular season championship, but now if we lost just one game in the Missouri Valley Conference tournament, we would have to sweat it out to see if we would get invited into the bracket.

The Valley tournament is one of the great traditions in college basketball. It has a lot of rich history. They call it "Arch Madness" because it is held in St. Louis. I may not have been turning handsprings anymore, but I wasn't about to miss this.

We got a scare in the first round from Northern Iowa, but after that the guys started to relax and play their games. They finished with a comfortable 65–49 win over Illinois State in the championship game. Just like that, the drought was over! We were going back to March Madness for the first time in thirty-three years.

One of the neat things about winning Arch Madness was that it made Porter only the second person in the history of the Valley to win the title as a player and a coach, because his Creighton team won it in 1989. When he was asked about that afterward, Porter smiled and said, "I'm going to be honest, it was probably more fun as a player."

Needless to say, I was overjoyed, but most of all I was thrilled for our players. When the game ended, they jumped and hugged and danced all over the court. That's exactly what you want to see from college kids who have just completed a major goal. When I was wheeled onto the court for the trophy presentation, the kids came up to me and gave me those big sweaty hugs that I love so much. Yes, we had more games to play, but those players had earned their chance to celebrate, and I was delighted to be able to celebrate right along with them.

Thirteen

The Sister Jean Bounce

*It only took me ninety-eight years to
become an overnight sensation.*

AS I ALWAYS DO before the start of the NCAA tournament, I
filled out a bracket. Normally no one cared who I picked, but because
Loyola was finally back in the Big Dance, a local TV station asked if
they could broadcast my picks. I picked the Ramblers to go all the
way to the Sweet Sixteen—I thought I was going out on a limb with
that one!

The day before we left for Dallas, I sat for an interview with CBS.
They sent a camera crew to Chicago to interview me, Porter, and
some of our players. I enjoyed the visit, but I didn't think much of it
at the time. Who would be interested in a ninety-eight-year-old nun
when the NCAA tournament was going on?

The NCAA provides chartered airplanes for all the teams in the tournament, which I think is wonderful. It gives these young guys a chance to stretch their legs. With their size, I don't know how some of them manage when they have to fly a regular commercial airline. I flew with the team to Dallas. The players and coaches sat up front, and the other passengers like me sat in the back. The hostesses took great care of us. I don't know if the coaches wanted the players to eat that unhealthy airplane food, but I devoured all of it.

When we got to Dallas, we were met with all the southern hospitality the city could muster. The people at the hotel were all wearing Loyola hats. Not all of our fans and students could make it to the next round of games, so the school set up a big watch party inside our student center. The kids were back from spring break, so the place was really packed. Many of our alumni came to watch as well.

And what a game they saw!

Our opponent was Miami. They were a No. 6 seed in the South region, and though they were in one of those leagues (the Atlantic Coast Conference) that always sent multiple teams to the tournament, their coach, Jim Larrañaga, was the coach of the Cinderella George Mason team that made the Final Four in 2006. So he understood that we could be dangerous. I did my usual prayer with the team in the hallway before the game and took my seat in the stands. I really thought we could win the game, but when we were down by five points with just under three minutes to play, I feared we were heading back to Chicago.

We made a terrific comeback but still trailed by one point heading into the closing seconds. Miami had a chance to go up by three with 9.6 seconds left but they missed a free throw. Ben got the rebound and immediately passed to Marques, who dribbled quickly upcourt. Marques could have taken the shot and tried to be the hero, but instead he passed it to Donte. Donte was a good five feet behind the three-point line, but because time was winding down he had to shoot it. It went in just as the final buzzer went off to give us the big *W.*

I thought my heart might explode! As soon as that ball went in, all our bench players ran onto the court and celebrated. It was pure youthful joy. That's what March Madness is all about. All those years of waiting to get back into the tournament were worth it to see that shot go in.

Everyone would remember that shot for a long time, but there was an unnoticed sequence late in the second half that defined what Loyola was all about. Porter wrote about it in his book *All In: Driven by Passion, Energy, and Purpose.* We were down seven points and Miami was about to put the game away when Ben ran downcourt and accidentally stepped on a referee's foot. He turned his ankle badly and crumpled to the floor. A moment later, Miami got the ball back and appeared to be headed for an easy basket. Ben jumped to his feet, ran as hard as he could on that injured ankle, stole the ball, and dished an assist to Marques. That basket totally changed the momentum of the game. It wasn't until a few minutes later when Ben was limping toward the huddle that Porter even realized he was hurt. We were all amazed at Ben's resilience.

Tom wheeled me onto the court as soon as the game ended. The players finished up their celebration and headed for the locker room. On their way off the court, each one stopped to hug me—sweaty hugs!—and share a few words. It's amazing to see the transformation that comes over the players in that moment. They're so excited, they're childlike. When they come off that court, you can see they're ready to scream. They get into the locker room and hug one another over and over.

Rosalyn Gold-Onwude, a sideline reporter who worked the game for TNT, came over and asked for my reaction. I didn't realize it at the time, but during the game Rosalyn had done a report on me, explaining to the audience who I was and what role I played for the team. "Oh, thank God, thank God we did it, because we knew we would do it," I said. "When we were in the locker room ahead of the game, we just knew that we would do this. Our team is so great and they don't care who makes the points as long as we win the game. I said we want to get the big *W* up there, and we did."

Rosalyn asked me if I saw any similarities between this team and our 1963 national champions. "Oh, I do because we share the ball," I said. "They don't care, they just share the ball. They have great teamwork and they're real good guys, and so was the team of sixty-three."

As I sat in my wheelchair outside the locker room, still flush with joy and excitement over the win, I noticed something weird was happening. Whenever I looked up, a photographer was aiming his or her lens at me and snapping away. A few reporters came up to me and asked me questions. A television reporter did the same with his camera crew. I couldn't help but chuckle at the thought that if this was back in the 1950s, I would have had to stay pretty much out of sight, because sisters weren't supposed to have their pictures taken. In 2018, however, I didn't have such restrictions, so I was free to soak it all up.

The celebration continued at the hotel. It wasn't easy to fall asleep. When I woke up the next morning, it took me a few seconds to recall where I was and what had happened. At first I wondered if it was all a dream. Then I snapped back to reality. *It wasn't a dream,* I thought to myself. *Time to get going.*

It wasn't long after my morning meditation that the phone in my hotel room rang. It was Bill Behrns, the head of communications for men's basketball at Loyola. He told me there was a reporter waiting for me in the lobby, and would I mind going down to speak with him. I said sure. I got dressed, went to the lobby, did the interview, and came back to my room. Then Bill called again and said he had someone else who wanted to speak with me. Thus began an exhilarating and exhausting day of riding that elevator up and down, up and down. It was a lot of riding and a *whole* lot of talking, but I never got tired. I loved talking about the Ramblers, and I wanted the whole world to appreciate what these kids had done.

So many interview requests were coming in that Bill had to assign someone on his staff to handle them all. It seemed they were always handing me a phone and asking me to speak to a reporter. I talked to the *New York Times,* the *Washington Post,* and lots of other media. *USA Today* called me "the most universally beloved fan during this year's NCAA tournament." All the sports shows were talking about Sister Jean and the Loyola Ramblers, and a lot of news shows were talking about us as well. I guess we were one of those stories that transcended sports. When I was wheeled through the lobby of our hotel or went to a restaurant to eat, people would shout my name and ask to take a selfie.

It only took me ninety-eight years to become an overnight sensation.

As excited as I was by all the attention, I would never let that interfere with my duties as chaplain. That meant meeting the team for the pregame prayer as usual. The difference this time was that I was wearing a microphone pack, and we were surrounded by cameras who recorded my message to the boys. "Don't let those Tennessee team members scare you with their height," I said in reference to our next opponent, the Tennessee Volunteers. "Height doesn't mean that much. You're good jumpers. You're good rebounders. You're good at everything, and just keep that in mind."

Our guys looked nervous at the start. Tennessee jumped out to a 15–6 lead, but once we settled down and made some baskets, the game became a real fight. We actually led by four points at halftime and with about three and a half minutes to play, we were up by nine. The game was tense, and as usual I calmed my nerves (and my stomach) by eating popcorn. At one point the TV cameras showed me watching intently while I popped that popcorn into my mouth. I was told later that that video became a popular gif on social media, although I'm not exactly sure what that means.

With twenty seconds to play, Tennessee took a one-point lead. We had one more chance, and fittingly it was seized by Clayton, who was our leading scorer and the player of the year in the Missouri Valley Conference. As the seconds ticked away, Clayton took a few dribbles and pulled up for a shot. It was short and hit the front of the rim. I've seen more balls hit that part of the rim than I could count, and they almost always bounce away. This time, however, the ball bounced *up*, hit high up on the backboard, hit the front of the rim again, and went through the hoop with 3.6 seconds to go. That gave Tennessee just enough time for one more shot, but they missed a three-pointer. The game was over! Loyola 63, Tennessee 62.

To say I was thrilled is the understatement of the century. My first thought when the game was over was to get down to that court as soon as possible. There was no way I was going to miss my sweaty hugs! The players celebrated with one another and shook hands with the Tennessee players. Then, one by one, they filed by my wheelchair and embraced me.

A few moments later, my new BFF, Rosalyn Gold-Onwude, came over with her microphone to ask me what I said to the team in my prayer before the game. "I told them that we were going to win, that we could do it and God would be on our side and we were just going to do it today," I said. "To keep calm and just put into play everything the coaches taught them to do."

She couldn't resist asking me about my bracket that had the Ramblers losing in the next round. "I just thought they would go to the Sweet Sixteen and now we may go even more than that," I said.

Everything was happening so fast. Of course, I had hoped and prayed that our team could win these games, but to see them do it was still quite a shock. And I certainly never expected that I would become such a big part of the story. Now I was seeing articles referring to our team as "Sister Jean's Ramblers." Even Chicago's most famous resident, Barack Obama, wrote a tweet saying, "Congrats to @LoyolaChicago and Sister Jean for a last-second upset—I had faith in my pick!"

Later, I was sitting outside the locker room when Clayton came out and hugged me again. I told him I didn't know if that ball was going to go in. "Sister Jean," he replied, "I didn't know either."

I've heard people say that Clayton's funky game winner went in because of a "Sister Jean bounce." That suggested that somehow my prayers made that ball defy the laws of gravity and go in. Is that true? Who's to say that it isn't? That's the beauty of God—we never really know what He's doing, or why. We have to trust Him to do His part, and then it's up to us to do ours. Those players worked hard for that victory. If it took a Sister Jean bounce to get us into the Sweet Sixteen, then that was a destiny worth celebrating.

Fourteen

The Final Four

*People called it a miracle, but I say
all the boxing out helped too.*

"I'M REALLY HAPPY TO be saying good morning to all of America today."

It was six thirty in the morning on Tuesday, March 20, 2018. I was sitting in my wheelchair at center court in Gentile Arena, looking into a TV camera while wearing my trademark Loyola scarf. (With the maroon and gold stripes, it is often compared to Harry Potter's scarf, which I take as a very nice compliment.) That morning I was doing an appearance on *Good Morning America* and speaking with the hosts back in New York City. This was a particular thrill for me because I like that show very much and I'm a big fan of George Stephanopoulos. I never miss his Sunday morning news show.

The possibility that I would be on *Good Morning America* would never have entered my mind one week before, but at that point it was very much in line with everything that was going on in my life. Ever since we had gotten back to Chicago, I felt like I had been caught in a hurricane—a wonderful, joyful, loving, godly hurricane. Bill Behrns told me his office had received nearly a hundred media requests for me. He and his assistant, Ryan Haley, did a wonderful job handling them all. They told me they said no to a lot of places, but it seemed to me like they said yes a lot too.

Here's what my Monday looked like: At 6 a.m., I hosted a camera crew from Chicago's CBS affiliate in my apartment at The Clare. That was followed by an interview with Chicago's WGN News. (Like many of the people I spoke with, the WGN anchor teased me that I had Loyola "only" going to the Sweet Sixteen in my bracket.) At 8:15 another camera crew, this one from ESPN, interviewed me at Loyola, and then I dialed into ESPN's *Golic and Wingo* show to do an interview along with Porter. "Without a doubt, I'm the luckiest coach in America," Porter told them. "I have an honorary assistant coach with direct divine intervention from above."

During the afternoon I did an interview over Skype with the TV show *Access Hollywood*. Then I did a third interview with ESPN, followed by yet another CBS interview. In between all those interviews I must have answered more than three hundred emails. The *New York Times* sent a reporter out to spend the day with me for an article that was published under the headline "A Day in the Life of Sister Jean, Media Darling."

And that was just Monday! Everywhere I looked, my image was being projected to the public. Some two dozen companies asked permission from Loyola to use my name and likeness on T-shirts, sweatshirts, signs, and even socks. The LEGOLAND Discovery Center in Chicago displayed a Sister Jean mini-figure that showed me dunking a basketball. Another Sister Jean bobblehead doll, this one manufactured by the National Bobblehead Hall of Fame and Museum, hit the market, and within forty hours it became the best-selling bobblehead in the museum's history. The attention was flattering, but I was acutely aware that the only reason people were talking about me was because of what the team had accomplished. I only hoped that with all of this going on, the players would be able to keep up with their studies.

The scene was even bigger when we got to Atlanta, where we were scheduled to play Nevada in the Sweet Sixteen. The team and I arrived there to great fanfare, especially when we rolled up to the hotel. Loyola had assigned a couple of security people to follow me around and protect me from well-wishers. I tried to tell them that wouldn't be necessary—"What am I, some kind of rock star?" I teased—but they insisted. I must admit, the security came in handy over the next few days.

One of the neatest interviews I did that week was with Mariah Musselman, the adorable daughter of Nevada coach Eric Musselman. She, too, had become a big celebrity as their team advanced to the Sweet Sixteen. So the TV networks thought it would be cute for the two of us to get together on camera.

Mariah was even more delightful in person than she was on TV. "Well, I guess it's just you and me today," I said as Tom wheeled me into the room. "How about that?" From there she lofted me a few questions:

Mariah: "What do you think about this matchup that's going down?"

Me: "I think it's going to be very good, and I know that we're going to have to work hard, and of course Nevada is going to have to work hard against us too. At least I feel that way, and you probably do too. I'm sure you're a little anxious about them. I said to our team the other day, I think I'm more nervous than you are."

Mariah: "You've gone viral. Do you know what that means?"

Me: "No. You'll have to tell me."

Mariah: "Going viral means you're *everywhere*. You're on the TV, you're on the internet."

Me: "I don't know how it all happened. It just all of a sudden came and you heard your name in lots of places, and people say hello to you and want your picture. So this is quite an experience for me, and it's probably going to go on with you the rest of your life."

We talked about good luck charms (I didn't have any, but she likes to wear wolf ears in honor of the Wolfpack), and then we exchanged shirts from our respective schools. "I think you and I are both blessed to have these teams and to be able to work with them and also know that these young men are good," I said. "They're good people. They're going to make an impact in the world. So it's a great pleasure for me to meet you today. We'll go into this together and we'll cheer for each other, and we have to live with whatever comes. We have to be good sports about it. The team has to be good sports, so you and I have to be good sports too."

Then we hugged. There we were, one very old lady and one very young lady, cheering for different teams but for the same reasons.

We wanted opposite outcomes, but we shared a common love for our teams and the people on them. That's what sports is supposed to be all about.

⌐

I can't say I've given much thought as to why I became such an object of fascination. Yes, our team was writing a Cinderella story, but that didn't have much to do with me. I think it starts with the fact that I'm so old. Let's face it, people love little old ladies! We're harmless, we're cheerful, and we've been through a few things. People innately want to be happy and safe—and stay alive.

But I'd also like to think people were interested in me because, whether they realized it or not, they wanted to be closer to God. They knew I had spent my whole life serving Him. We hear so much about the negative aspects of human nature, but my ride through the 2018 NCAA tournament revealed just how much goodness there is in people. I hope we never lose sight of that.

Eventually, it was time to play the game. Once again, I wore a microphone and was trailed by TV cameras for the pregame prayer. As the boys held hands with me and one another and formed a circle, I sensed they were a little more nervous than usual. "Are you ready to play?" I said with a smile, hoping to lighten the mood. They responded yes, and then I went into my prayer:

"Good and gracious God, as we gather to beat that pack of wolves, stay focused, use your heads and your hearts, and let's make that next game our Elite Eight. God bless us, go Ramblers, and amen!"

Our fans were ready. One of them held up a big sign with my

picture on it beneath the words "Mission from God." When the game finally tipped off, I could hardly sit still. I don't know what it was about our guys—maybe they liked torturing me?—but once again they were nervous and got off to a bad start, falling behind by twelve points during the first ten minutes. After that we were on fire and took a 28–24 halftime lead. I noticed during the game that the fans from Kansas State and Kentucky, who were there to watch their teams play in the second game, were cheering like mad for us. We had become America's darlings. I also noticed that Coach Musselman had even more nervous energy on the sideline than Porter. I didn't think that was possible.

Our best player that night was Marques, which was great considering he didn't play so well the first two rounds. He led us in scoring with eighteen points, and he hit the biggest shot of the night when he made a three-pointer with 6.3 seconds to play to give us a 69–68 win. Amazingly, we had won our three NCAA tournament games by a total of four points. Clayton actually had a chance to take the big shot, but he sensed that Marques was hot, so he got him the ball instead. Once again, Clayton showed that he was a great team player.

As he ran off the court, Clayton hugged me and shouted, "Sister Jean, we busted your bracket!" I've never been so happy to be so wrong!

After the game, Porter was asked about a lineup change he made at the start of the second half. He said that in the locker room at halftime, his assistant, Bryan Mullins, had suggested they start Aundre Jackson instead of Cameron Krutwig. Aundre was smaller, but Nevada wasn't a big team, and Bryan thought it would give us more quickness. Porter agreed to try it, and it worked. Giving Bryan credit was a great example of Porter being a team player—of sharing the ball, so to speak. As a result of Porter's remark, the *Chicago Tribune* published a story on Bryan the following week, and a year later Bryan was hired to be the head coach at his alma mater, Southern Illinois.

As I was waiting outside the locker room, I was surrounded by reporters. "I'm happy for us, for my community, for Loyola, for the city of Chicago, and for the world," I told them, "because we have people watching us all over the world. The viewing numbers on every channel should go up over this weekend, and I'm sure that it will."

A few feet away, my friend Mariah Musselman passed Clayton and asked, "Will you apologize to my dad for beating us?"

Clayton smiled and said, "No, but I'll apologize to you."

I was especially pleased that four members of our 1963 championship team—Jerry Harkness, Les Hunter, John Egan, and Rich Rochelle—were on hand for the big win. They were there again two days later for our Elite Eight game against Kansas State, which I'm happy to say was a *lot* more boring. It's a good thing, too, because I don't know that my heart could have taken another buzzer beater. I was able to enjoy the second half as our boys finished with a 78–62 win. Tom wheeled me onto the court for my sweaty hugs, and I had a great view as one Rambler after another climbed the ladder and cut down the net commemorating our regional championship.

As I looked around the arena and soaked up the moment, I had to shake my head. Loyola University was going to the Final Four for the first time since 1963. We were indeed on a mission from God. People called it a miracle, but I say all the boxing out helped too.

You can imagine what the next few days were like back home in Chicago. I went through another hurricane of interviews, spent hours returning phone calls and emails, and took more selfies than I could count. A few reporters even traveled to the motherhouse in Dubuque, where the sisters had my bobblehead doll on display. They were delighting in my turn as an international celebrity and said they were rooting real hard for Loyola. I loved the attention, not for my ego but because I loved meeting people and talking about my team. I wanted so badly for those boys to keep winning.

The Final Four was held in San Antonio, and everything about the experience was bigger—the crowds, the hotels, the stadium, the excitement. When we got to the hotel, we were greeted by scores of Loyola signs all over the property. The whole lobby was decked in maroon and gold. It was just like being at home, except wherever we went, photographers were clicking and cameras were flashing all over the place.

As it turned out, I wasn't the only little old lady with a rooting interest in our game against Michigan. The grandmother of Jalen Rose, who was one of the famous "Fab Five" that played for Michigan in the early 1990s, put out a video on Instagram and said, "Sister Jean, it's been a good ride. But it's over Saturday. Go Blue!" You gotta respect an old lady who knows how to talk some trash!

Michigan's coach, John Beilein, said he was doing all he could to match the advantage that people said I was bringing to Loyola. "I have heard from many religious people that I personally know that tell me their prayers are doing everything they can to counter Sister Jean," he said.

Of all the things I experienced during this glorious time, the most amazing (outside of the games, of course) was my Friday press conference at the Alamodome. The place was packed! I went up to the dais and poured my heart out. "This is the most fun I've had in my life," I said. "I never even imagined two or three people being here, let alone this large group. Everything just seemed to mushroom, and I could never tell you how that happens. It's a big thrill for me to be here this morning with all of you, and you know what? I'm not a bit nervous."

The reporters were very polite as they asked me a range of questions, starting with whether I had seen the video of Jalen Rose's grandmother. "I saw it on Facebook the other day," I said. "I also heard that she said she's out to get me, so we'll see. Somebody said, 'Maybe you need a pair of boxing gloves,' and I said, 'Well, we'll see what happens.' I hope we see each other. I hope we meet there. I love to meet people."

I was asked, Is God a basketball fan? "He probably is, and he's probably a basketball fan more of the NCAA than the NBA. I'll wager that your viewer audience is very large this time and that if you compare it to the NBA when they're playing, it will be different. And I say that because these young people are playing with their hearts and not for any financial assistance."

What did I think about all the attention I was getting? "I'm amazed at what the different channels and radio stations and all the reporters from all the papers and so forth do. And when they say, 'I came in from New York to do this,' like three or four photographers, and I think to myself, 'Oh my, don't let it go to your head.' I haven't done that, nor has the team. The team, those young men are very humble."

One reporter, noting it was Good Friday, asked what I thought it would take for someone to have their prayers heard by God, especially if they're praying for their team to win. "Well, it all depends on how hard you work for it. We have a little slogan that we say: Worship, work, and win. And so, you need to do all those things. God always hears but maybe He thinks it's better for us to get the *L* instead of the *W,* and we have to accept that."

I ended by saying to the reporters, "You're great people, and don't let anybody put you down at any time." When it was over, they gave me a round of applause. Who says reporters are cynical?

There was so much buildup, I almost wondered if the game would ever arrive. Finally, Saturday night came. I got a big ovation when Tom wheeled me to my spot near the court. There were nearly seventy thousand people in the Alamodome. One of the highlights for me was meeting Charles Barkley, who was part of the broadcast team for CBS and Turner Sports. Charles was very charming and I thanked him for saying hello. I added, "I loved watching you play, but you didn't smile enough." I think I embarrassed him a bit, but he knew I was right. Greg Gumbel of CBS also came over to say hello. He reminded me that I taught his sister, Rhonda, at Mundelein. "I know!" I shouted over the crowd noise. "I think of her every time I see you!" He was shocked that I remembered.

Finally, the game got underway, and our boys were magnificent. Michigan was a No. 3 seed in their region, and since it was in the Big Ten it's rightly considered to be a powerhouse program. We were with them every step of the way, and early in the second half we held a ten-point lead. Unfortunately, we couldn't hang on, and we ended up losing, 69–57.

Our players were devastated because they felt like they should have won the game. Many of them came over to hug me, and this time the sweat was mixed with some tears. I liked that they weren't just "happy to be there," but true to form, they showed total class and great sportsmanship in defeat, giving credit to Michigan and showing appreciation for what they had accomplished. Michigan was classy in victory as well. As I was being wheeled down a hallway, one of their best players, Jordan Poole, rushed over, shook my hand, and said, "I just want to say I'm a big fan of you guys. Congratulations."

With all the talking I had done, it didn't occur to me that any reporter would still want to ask me questions, especially considering we had lost. Several of them went up to Ryan Haley to ask if they could speak with me, but he politely shooed them away. "She's done for a while," he said. "We're going to give her a little bit of an extended break from everything and let her kind of catch her breath."

I would have been happy to say a few parting words, but I appreciated Ryan looking out for me. And truth be told, he was right. I was exhausted but also exhilarated and appreciative for all God had done for me and the Ramblers. It was bittersweet to see the season come to an end, but we knew that something special had happened that people would never forget. The scoreboard may have said that Michigan had more points than we did that night, but there was no doubt in my mind that we left that court as winners.

Fifteen

Wins and Losses, Hellos and Goodbyes

On our campus, the big name is Loyola.

WHEN WE ARRIVED BACK in Chicago, a squad of police cars was waiting to escort our bus back to campus. I could see maroon and gold decorations all over the city, and there was a terrific crowd awaiting our arrival. No one expressed any disappointment that we had not gone all the way as the 1963 team did. They were just appreciative of what we had accomplished—as were we.

The celebrations lasted through the spring. I accompanied the team on a trip to Springfield, Illinois, so they could be honored by our governor. I got a real thrill when I was invited to throw out the first pitch at a Cubs game. I was wearing a Cubs jacket and maroon Loyola ski cap when Tom wheeled me onto the field. Then

I stood up and fired a ninety-mile-an-hour strike right down the middle. (Okay, so I tossed it underhanded and it bounced harmlessly through the dirt, but give an old nun a chance to dream, won't you?) My hometown—San Francisco—established a Sister Jean Day, and I was featured in several Catholic magazines around the country. I didn't even know about many of those stories until people mailed me copies. Each morning my email inbox brought me a steady stream of messages from friends and strangers across the globe thanking me for what I had done. It was all very fulfilling and kept me in God's spirits, that's for sure.

A few days after we got home from the Final Four, I was asked to go over to Gentile Arena to meet with a couple of recruits. When I got there, Porter asked me to step outside for a moment. He told me that he had been invited to interview for the head coaching job at Saint John's University in New York City. He was giving me the courtesy of letting me know, but he also wanted my advice. I encouraged him to write down a list of all the pros and cons so he could factor in every aspect of this decision. That started with his family. Porter has always done a remarkable job of balancing his work and family life, which unfortunately can't be said for a lot of college basketball coaches. I wrote him an email that night laying out some pertinent questions. At the end of the letter I asked simply, "Do you truly want the new job?"

Porter tried to keep his trip to New York quiet, but someone recognized him on campus, and before long word reached Loyola that he was considering this move. Porter's family had given him free rein to make the decision. He knew they loved Loyola and living in Chicago, but this was a big opportunity that needed to be fully considered. Porter knew that I would not hold it against him if he wanted to go. I loved having him as our coach, but I wanted him to do what was best for him, not me. I've spent my whole life encouraging young people to follow their dreams. I wanted the same thing for Porter.

He was genuinely torn about what he should do. Porter took my advice about the pros and cons list to a higher level. On the flight home from New York, he wrote two letters to Rambler Nation. The first one announced he was leaving, the second announced he was staying. He read each one and discerned how they made him feel. Then he prayed. He decided he felt a lot better about the letter announcing he was staying. So he told Saint John's no thank you and prepared for another season with the Ramblers.

The excitement of the Final Four carried our campus through the end of the school year. Even when the students were gathered in study groups for final exams, everyone seemed unusually chipper. I would roll by and ask why they were so happy. "Oh, Sister Jean, the Final Four!" they replied. How silly of me to ask.

As proud as I was of our team for making the Final Four, I was even more proud when I learned that our men's basketball team had the number one graduation rate in the entire country that season. Now *that's* a big *W.*

I thought I was making progress with my rehabilitation and looked forward to getting out of that wheelchair once and for all. But I encountered a major setback over the summer when I got shingles. Though it is very uncomfortable on the skin, even worse, it does a lot of damage to your nerves and muscles. I had to work even harder at my rehabilitation to strengthen my leg. That included getting Botox injections every three months to liven up the nerves and restore the muscles. I like to tell people I have the best-looking foot in the world because of all those Botox injections.

Though I was disappointed, in time I had another basketball season to look forward to. Three of our starters from the Final Four team would be returning, and Lucas Williamson was ready to step into his role on the starting five. A big challenge for Porter was to make sure his players didn't get too full of themselves. You could hardly blame them after they were showered with so much attention and praise. But Porter's motto for the program was "no excuses, no complaining, no entitlement." The team may have gone to the Final Four, but Porter made sure that on the first day of school the basketball players were right there to help the freshmen move into their dorms, just like always.

The notion of service is a very important part of our program and our school in general. A few years ago the players started working with Misericordia, a local organization that cares for people with severe disabilities. Every year the team hosts a "Misericordia night," where the disabled community comes to a game and cheers on the Ramblers. As was the case with SMILE, the idea of this program was to help the folks with disabilities, but Porter and his coaches understood the great benefits the players would enjoy from knowing they were helping other people.

Even though we were going to miss the three seniors who graduated, we were getting a boost from the addition of Aher Uguak, a six-foot-seven sophomore who sat out the previous season after transferring from New Mexico. Aher was born in Egypt after his family had to flee their native South Sudan because of civil war, but when he was eight months old they moved to Canada. I thought he was quite shy when he first came in and not very aggressive on the court, but it didn't take long for his competitiveness to come out.

Complacency was never a problem with this group. If anything, the team was *too* intent on living up to the Final Four expectations. It was not fair considering how hard it is for any team, much less one at our level, to make the Final Four even once. At one point Porter had to tell Clayton Custer, who was now a senior, that he was required to smile at him three times during practice. Basketball is supposed to be fun, but sometimes it's easy to forget that. (It's easy to forget that about a lot of things, come to think of it.)

And yet, through all of that, our boys played great and won the Missouri Valley Conference regular season championship. Unfortunately, our season ended when we lost, 53–51, to Bradley in the semifinals at Arch Madness. We had beaten Bradley the previous year in the tournament, so I'm pretty sure they were happy about getting their revenge. We ended up playing in the National Invitation Tournament, where we lost in the first round to Creighton, Porter's alma mater. It was a tough way to end the season, but I'm proud to report that the team posted an overall grade point average of 3.48. At Loyola, our student-athletes take their studies very seriously.

The summer of 2019 marked yet another significant occasion: my one-hundredth birthday, on August 21. I was honored by Illinois governor J. B. Pritzker, who declared it "Sister Jean Day" across the entire state. (Live a hundred years, you get yourself a day!) The LEGOLAND Discovery Center commissioned a statue of me, this one standing two and a half feet tall and consisting of more than ten thousand LEGO bricks. That summer the school also completed the Alfie Norville Practice Facility. It was a great accomplishment, not to mention a huge boon for recruiting.

One of the new arrivals that year was Marquise Kennedy, a six-foot-one freshman guard from Brother Rice High School in Chicago. One of the reasons Porter recruited him was because on his visit, every time someone held open a door for Marquise, he looked the person in the eye and said thank you. That showed Porter that he was a young man of great character. Once again, we had a solid season, this time finishing second in the conference. We played Valparaiso in our first game at Arch Madness and sprinted out to a fourteen-point lead at halftime. Alas, we fell apart in the second half and ended up losing in overtime, 74–73. Oh, that was a blow! I'll never forget the look on Porter's face as he came off the court. He was just devastated, and the team felt the same way.

As it turned out, we were lucky to be able to play the game at all. The coronavirus pandemic had been building since January, and it had gotten so bad that the following week, all the conference tournaments were canceled. Then the NCAA tournament was canceled. It was a very sad and scary time, for us and the entire world.

The pandemic forced colleges around the country to conduct online learning, and all public events, including sports, were shut down through the summer. I felt so sorry for our seniors who would not get a proper graduation ceremony. It was hard on all the parents, too, because a lot of students went home to finish up their school year. Nobody had ever faced anything like this, and we weren't sure what to do. The hardest part was the way young kids were not able to be with their friends.

Naturally, I was frightened of getting the virus myself, but thankfully the people at The Clare did a great job keeping us isolated and safe. And believe me, I kept plenty busy. I stayed in constant communication with people through email and the phone, checking in on all the programs that I helped to run. That included students I knew at Arrupe College, which is our two-year institution. I also wrote to students in the ACE program, which stands for Achieving College Excellence. I knew they were going through their own challenges because of the pandemic, and I wanted to make them feel at home. I find that when we are sad, helping other people overcome their own sadness makes us feel a lot better.

I know that many people, especially older people, experienced depression during that time, but I did not. Sure, I was frustrated, and I worried about what was going on all over the world with this terrible virus. But I've never been depressed. I am lucky that I came from a happy home. I've had a happy life. I enjoy what I do. There's nothing for me to be depressed about.

During the pandemic, I put a big priority on staying in touch with the Ramblers. I emailed the team frequently and called the players to check in. Someone came in and taught me how to do a Zoom call on my iPad. As busy as I was, I always set aside some time at three thirty every afternoon to watch *Jeopardy*. That was my daily reward.

The online learning continued throughout the summer and into the school year. College sports was able to resume in the fall, but the players were under strict guidelines to stay isolated, and they were tested frequently. What a sacrifice they made! No fans were allowed at the games, but I watched them on television, and when they weren't on TV I followed the action on my iPad. I couldn't do the pregame prayers in person, so I delivered them over a speakerphone, and I continued to send my scouting reports. It turned out to be another memorable season. We rolled through the Missouri Valley Conference again, and by the middle of February we were back in the national rankings.

We had been neck and neck with Drake all season, so it was fitting that we played them in the championship game of Arch Madness. All the "bracketologists" were saying that even if we lost that game we would still be in the NCAA tournament, but our boys wanted to remove all doubt. I delivered my usual pregame prayer over speakerphone, and then they beat Drake, 75–65, to capture another conference tournament title. As soon as our game was over, one of the TV announcers predicted that our team was capable of making another run to the Final Four. He added, "I've got four words for you, America: Get Sister Jean vaccinated!"

He was referring to the COVID-19 vaccine, which had come out in December and was slowly working its way to the public. I thought it was a miracle and a godsend. Since I am, shall we say, of an advanced age, I was among the first to get the vaccine when it became available in February. By the time the NCAA tournament rolled around I was all set. Instead of being held at various sites around the country, the tournament was held in a "bubble" in Indianapolis. A small number of fans and family would be allowed to attend. There was no way I was going to let my Ramblers take the court without my being there.

Because of all the restrictions, I could not be around the team, so I had to continue to deliver my pregame messages via speakerphone. I sat in the upper level wearing my Loyola mask as we won our first-round game against Georgia Tech. That set up a matchup against Illinois. The game was huge for many reasons. The first was that the winner got to go to the Sweet Sixteen. Illinois was also a No. 1 seed, so they were the heavy favorite. And of course, they were our in-state rivals. We rarely played Illinois during the regular season—maybe they're afraid to play us?—so this was our chance to show we could beat our big brothers.

I spent extra time scouting Illinois beforehand. I wanted to have the best possible information for the team for the prayer. "As we play the Fighting Illini, we ask for special help to overcome this team and get a great win," I told them. "We hope to score early and make our opponents nervous. We have a great opportunity to convert rebounds as this team makes about 50 percent of layups and 30 percent of its three-point shots. Our defense can take care of that."

Wouldn't you know, that is exactly what happened. Illinois only made 45 percent of its shots and shot 29 percent from three-point land, and we pulled out the 71–58 win. It may have been technically an upset, but by then people had learned to stop thinking of Loyola as Cinderella. My favorite part of the day was when Cameron Krutwig, who by that time had become one of the best players in Loyola history, was doing an interview with the broadcast network after the game while wearing a headset. He was midsentence when the rest of the players ran over to him and started hugging and dancing together. The announcers were happy to have their interview interrupted. After all those kids had been through, they deserved to celebrate any way they wanted.

For our Sweet Sixteen game against Oregon State, we were in

the unusual position of favorite. We were a No. 8 seed, but they were a No. 12 seed, which is even lower than we were when we made the Final Four two years before. Sure enough, the underdog won again, and our season was over.

When we got back to Chicago, Porter let me know he was considering another offer, this one from the University of Oklahoma. I could tell right away that he was considering it very seriously. Oklahoma is a prominent state school, and Porter sounded as though he was excited about the chance to do great things there. This time he accepted the job. A few days later, Loyola promoted his top assistant, Drew Valentine, to the head coaching spot.

Drew was only twenty-nine years old, making him the youngest coach in the country. Some people didn't like that we were hiring someone so young, much less someone who had never been a head coach before. They wanted us to go out and get a "big name" coach. But on our campus, the big name is *Loyola*. I had no doubt that Drew was 100 percent prepared for the job.

I wanted to give Porter a proper going-away present. When he was settled into his new office at Oklahoma, he received a package from me containing a book I had put together of all the emails, prayers, and messages I had written to him during his last season at Loyola. Porter's coaching at LU had the longest tenure that any head coach had enjoyed since George Ireland retired in 1975. Porter called me to say thanks for the gift. I again wished him all the best in his new job and thanked him for leaving the program in such good hands. That's the thing about life and basketball. They're both full of wins and losses, hellos and goodbyes. Porter had done wonderful work during his time at Loyola. Now it was time for the program to start a new chapter.

Sixteen

That Old Community Spirit

We can put on whatever costume we want, but
God sees who we really are on the inside.

A JOURNALISM MAJOR AT Loyola once said she wanted to interview me about all the changes I've seen over the years. I asked her how long she needed, and she said fifteen minutes. "Fifteen minutes?" I replied. "If I give you one minute for every year of my life, we would miss dinner."

I'm sure it's hard for young people today to imagine a time when the only place to get the news was through newspapers. When I was growing up in San Francisco, we had a morning paper and an evening paper, and when something exciting happened they would print an "extra." The young paperboy would be walking down the street yelling, "Extra! Extra!" just like you see in the movies. My dad would give us two pennies so we could buy one.

Our student newspaper is called the *Loyola Phoenix*. The students who work there are really special. I'm telling you, they could be investigators on any news channel. Don't let anyone tell you that young people today don't want to work. Those student reporters are diggers. They know how to get the job done.

I am very intentional about staying on top of the news. I am a regular watcher of ABC's *World News Tonight* with David Muir. I don't like it as much when they have a substitute anchor, but I understand he needs a break once in a while. On Sunday I watch George Stephanopoulos. I used to be an avid reader of the Chicago newspapers, but they've taken a hit economically the last few years. I read parts of the *New York Times* on my computer every morning, and I have other news sources I access on my iPad.

I understand it's very hard today to convey the news properly and fairly. It falls to all of us to make an extra effort to ensure that what we are reading is true. Older folks like me are especially susceptible to being fooled because we are typically not comfortable using technology. And it's not just the news that's a challenge. I must get five calls a day from people asking for money. I don't even know how they get my number. Usually I don't even answer the phone, but I don't know how many people my age understand that and end up getting scammed.

I believe this is why so many people didn't want to get the COVID vaccine—there was so much conflicting and false information. I thought that was unfortunate, not to mention dangerous. There is also misinformation with respect to climate change. Although evidence suggests it is a serious problem, many don't believe it's happening. Our planet is one of God's most beautiful gifts to humanity, and I pray that we will do a much better job taking care of it. With all the contradictory information out there, it is wise for us to pay attention to what's actually true.

⁓

The 2021–2022 basketball season marked a new chapter in Loyola basketball history, but it also featured a look back to a vital part of our past. That light came in the form of a documentary about our 1963 championship team. It was important for people to learn this history, not just because of how great that team was, but because of the racial barriers those players helped to dismantle. This was especially important in the wake of the murder of George Floyd in 2020, which was one of the most tragic things I had ever witnessed. That incident set off a wave of Black Lives Matter protests, which reminded me very much of the protest movements of the sixties.

We had showings of the documentary on campus, and all the living members of that team did interviews and took part in panel discussions. My favorite part of the documentary was that Lucas Williamson narrated it. He did a marvelous job, as did the producers.

Sports has always been one of the best places for social progress to be made. It's a simple formula: if you want to win the game, you have to put your best players out there, regardless of their race. That's why I love athletes so much. If they have differences, they're going to say it to one another and talk it through, even if that means arguing about it. It's okay to argue with your teammates, just like we argue with our families. The important thing is to keep your eye on the main goal—to win.

Little kids understand this best of all. Many of you may have seen the video that went viral of the little Black boy and the little white boy running toward each other and hugging. (See, Mariah? I know what "viral" means now.) They had no idea they were looking at someone who was different—because they weren't. I thought what was interesting about that video was not just the actions of those darling little boys but how so many who saw the video then shared it with their friends. It speaks to the deep yearning we have to connect with our fellow human. This is what God wishes for us, but He can only do so much.

It's incredible to think that not that long ago there were parts of this country that thought it should be illegal for white people to play a basketball game against Black people. I'm glad we've come so far, but I also understand that in many areas of our society we still have a long way to go. I'd like to think that learning about our past can help people—especially young people—find a path forward where everyone is treated equally.

Loyola is often accurately referred to as a Jesuit school, but it is also a diverse, welcoming community. For example, we have one of the largest Muslim populations of any university in the country. One of my good friends on the faculty is Omer Mozaffar, the Muslim chaplain at our Division of Mission Integration. Omer teaches classes on scripture, student life, and other subjects. I was gratified when Omer wrote an article about our relationship and said, "In seeking to be a home for all faiths, Loyola employs me to nurture students because of my Islam, not despite it." He's the Division's version of Sister Jean, only without the hype sneakers.

Our Muslim population has enriched our community in so

many ways. I formed a particularly close friendship with a young Muslim student named Wesam Shahed. His parents had moved to Chicago from the Middle East before Wesam was born. Wesam was a junior when we first met, and he wanted to be a resident advisor. As part of the RA training program, each resident participated in a raffle. He won second prize, which was to have dinner with me. I found out later that Wesam felt a little nervous at first. He was a young Muslim man, and I was an old Catholic nun. How would we bridge those gaps? Would the conversation be awkward? Within the first few minutes of our meal, those differences melted away, as they always do.

We talked about our backgrounds, our families, and most of all, our love for the Ramblers. Then Wesam dropped a big surprise on me: *he* was the school mascot at the basketball games. The LU Wolf! The dinner was so delightful, Wesam asked if we could do it again sometime.

From that point on, we met at least once a month. Wesam would push my wheelchair across campus and through the dining hall. He brought me to his residence hall so I could individually bless all the rooms. People would tease him that they thought I was his grandma. It was a cute joke, except of course I looked far too young to be his grandma.

The games were especially fun. Wesam would be wearing the Lu costume, plop down next to me, and say, "Guess who." We made quite the pair, let me tell you. The fans would line up around the court at halftime to get their pictures taken with us.

Wesam went on to attend law school at Michigan State. When they heard about his background, they asked if he would dress up as their school mascot, Sparky, for the games. Wesam was flattered but said he was too busy. I thought that was a sign of progress. The old Wesam would have gobbled up the opportunity to be a mascot, even if it came at the expense of his studies.

Wesam and I remain in very close touch. During a recent visit he brought me a rosary from his aunt who lives in Israel. I still keep it in my room. I was gratified to teach Wesam many important lessons, but he taught me a lot too. We each helped the other understand that there's no reason to put up barriers between ourselves and other people, no matter our differences in age, gender, race, or religion. We can put on whatever costume we want, but God sees who we really are on the inside. And we're all the same in His eyes.

I'm inspired and gratified when I see how well our students understand this concept. I'm sure it's a big reason they came to Loyola in the first place. Lots of people say they are for equality, but in 2015 our students put their money where their mouths were and voted to contribute five dollars from their student fees each semester to form a scholarship fund for undocumented students who were not eligible for state or federal financial aid. The referendum passed with 70 percent voting yes. Five bucks is not a lot of money, but they were stating an important principle as well. "It says, 'Here at Loyola we accept the best and the brightest no matter what their documentation is,'" the student body president, Flavio Bravo, told the *Loyola Phoenix*. Loyola's Latin American Student Organization worked with the office of financial assistance to oversee the scholarship program and award the money.

The newspapers picked up what the students were doing, and as a result of the publicity someone from New York donated $50,000 to the scholarship fund. If there was any controversy or blowback from this, I didn't hear of it. There was no government money involved, so there was no reason for anyone to complain. A couple of years later, the students decided to increase their contributions to ten dollars per semester.

This was a perfect example of the "liberation theology" the Jesuits have always practiced. I understand people are concerned about how many immigrants are coming to America, legally and illegally, but I firmly believe these new arrivals need to be educated. There's an old saying that if you educate a woman, you educate a village. I would say the same about a man. This is not just an act of charity either. Some of these people are scholars. I think it would be shortsighted for us to say we don't need them. A lot of them are willing to do work that Americans consider too lowly. I don't believe there is such a thing as a "lowly" job. Every job is important in God's eyes.

I worry that we have lost much of our community spirit, and I pray often that we can find it again. I felt the loss of this spirit when I heard about all the fighting over wearing masks during the COVID pandemic. Many people said they didn't want to wear the masks because they were young and healthy and wouldn't get too sick from COVID. Maybe that's true, but that discounts the fact that masks were helpful in preventing *other* people from getting COVID—people like me who were older and much more likely to get incredibly sick from the virus.

The spirit of connectedness is yet another reason why I love going to basketball games. That is one place where people of all races, religions, and beliefs come together for one common purpose—to cheer on the Ramblers. So I was very glad that enough progress had been made with the virus to allow fans back in the arena for Drew Valentine's first season as coach. One of my favorite parts of the home games is the "Jesuit Jam." This is where a group of students who are studying to become priests do a dance on the court before the games with musical chairs and all kinds of fun stuff. They've made some amazing videos, which you can see on YouTube.

The excitement on campus was palpable when the students returned for the fall of 2021. I told our administrators that I thought this was the happiest freshman class we'd ever had. I didn't have any data or surveys to back this up, but I knew what I was seeing.

Even so, I know the pandemic hit young people hard, and that many of them were still struggling psychologically with the long-term effects. Our wellness center on campus remained very busy, and oftentimes it was filled with students who came in for mental health reasons. The wellness center building has an office that provides all kinds of assistance, including financial administration, so if a person walks in there, others don't know the reason they've come. That's a good thing, but I also think it's a good thing that universities and sports teams are being more proactive when it comes to talking about and treating mental health. For too long there has been a stigma around this, and I am glad to see that changing.

It's important for us to collectively address our problems, but I also believe we don't talk enough about all the good things that are happening. Yes, we have some students at Loyola who are struggling, but we also have thousands of students who are thriving. We should be talking about them, too, and giving them just as much of our love and attention.

I'm also happy to report that student activism is alive and well.

I'm glad that students are so engaged in issues that go well beyond campus, but I'm afraid that too many college communities have become intolerant of different opinions. If a college invites someone to give a guest lecture whom the students don't like, they will often try to get that person disinvited. However, I believe that even if someone says a lot of things we disagree with, oftentimes it's worth hearing them out. Maybe they'll say ninety-nine things you don't like, but then they'll say one or two things you do like, and it gets you thinking in a different direction. Young people tend to forget—if they even knew in the first place—that many of our greatest leaders started off quite unpopular. People claimed they were saying awful things, but over time—sometimes after they were no longer alive—we came to appreciate what they were trying to tell us.

College students have access to so much information these days, they have the ability to make change and get involved. But if you're only willing to shout at people and not listen to them, you'll never be able to bring them over to your side. I remember one day a group of students walked into the Damen Student Center and were protesting on behalf of a cause. They walked right into the main study area carrying their signs and shouting their slogans. Some of the students in that room might have agreed with their point of view, but they were there to do their work, and the protesters had interrupted their quiet. So instead of joining the protesters in support of their cause, the students packed up their backpacks and went elsewhere to study. I appreciated that those protesters felt so strongly, but they certainly didn't win any converts that day.

Here in downtown Chicago, we are faced with the reality of gun violence on a regular basis. It is frightening and frustrating, and also incredibly sad. We're not too far from Highland Park, where they recently had a tragic shooting during the Fourth of July parade. Those big shootings get a lot of attention, but similar tragedies are happening all over the streets of our great city. I wish I could better understand why we're the only country where this seems to be happening.

When events like 9/11 or the Highland Park shooting happen, it's natural to ask, *Where is God in all of this*? I don't pretend to know all of God's ways and His reasonings, but I know He's not the one making those things happen. I think these situations make God very sad. Maybe He's trying to teach us something about the need for all of us to get along better. People always ask why God lets these things happen, but we need to remember that He let bad things happen back in the Old Testament too. God created us in His image, and He gave us the ability to choose right from wrong. I don't think He wants to be fixing all of our problems all the time. That's what faith is supposed to be all about. It's easy to say, "Thank You, God" when your favorite basketball team gets the big *W.* But can you turn to God in your worst moments? When all you see are violence and despair? Maybe those are the questions that God is asking. We can pray all we want, but I also believe that we have to do our part.

I was 102 years old when the 2021–2022 season tipped off. The Ramblers gave Drew their best efforts, and as a result he had a banner first season. For one week in January we even made the national rankings again. If there's a downside to all this winning, it's that our fans expected it to continue automatically. They forgot how hard everyone had to work just to get to this point.

Fans and the alumni are the most critical people in the world. I want to say to them, "It's not so easy. Even Michael Jordan said when your legs are tired, it's hard to shoot a free throw." I've seen that fatigue get to our kids both physically and mentally. That's why when they roll me up to the court to watch the games, I ask to be put in a spot where the person on the foul line can't see me so easily. I don't want to make anyone nervous.

I went to all the home games and as many road games as I could that season. For the ones I couldn't attend, I watched on TV or followed the play-by-play on my iPad or computer. I've got a pretty good computer, but it's old—like me. It's quite stressful when we aren't playing well because I know what we are capable of.

We finished second in the Missouri Valley Conference and won Arch Madness to reach the NCAA tournament for the third time in five years, which was incredible considering that before that we had missed out on thirty-three straight tournaments. Drew was the last one to climb the ladder to cut down the championship net. He clipped an extra strand, turned to the people on the floor, and shouted, "For Sister Jean!" Then he climbed down and presented me with a piece of the net.

You'd think I'd be old news by now (pardon the pun), but once again I was blessed with a hurricane of Sister Jean stories as the 2022 NCAA tournament approached. I did round after round of telephone and television interviews. Jimmy Fallon even referenced me during his monologue on *The Tonight Show*. They put up fake tweets that had me saying things like, "I'm #turnt to watch my Gucci fam pound these dank opps in the paint, and simp bougie teams like Yale get smoked, no cap."

Loosely translated, I believe that means, "Go Ramblers!"

Our team was sent to Pittsburgh for the first round, and I went there right along with them. When a reporter from *USA Today* asked what I would say to the team before the game, I replied, "I always tell them this, I tell them they have to play with their mind and their heart and their hands and their feet. They say, 'Sister Jean, why our feet?' Because you have to get those fast breaks and just go!"

This time when I filled out my bracket, I had us going all the way to the Elite Eight. Nothing would have pleased me more than to have the boys bust my bracket again, but unfortunately, we lost our first game to Ohio State, bringing to a close another thrilling season.

Seventeen

Getting Old and Staying Young

Sometimes I think my life is just one big selfie.

ONE OF THE GREAT things about what I do is I never know the impact I've had on a student. One small comment said to the right person in the right place at the right time can make a huge difference.

I was recently sitting in my office and a young man came to visit. "Sister Jean, I just wanted to thank you for what you said to me when I was a freshman," he said. "I was sitting at a table all alone and feeling sorry for myself. You came over and talked to me and asked me how I was doing and what I was studying. I said I wanted to be a doctor, but that I didn't feel school was going well. You really encouraged me and gave me so much confidence, and now I'm in my third year of medical school."

I had no recollection of that conversation. I have them all the time. It's my constant drumbeat with these kids: *Don't spoil your dream! Go for it!* Young people tend to be very open and honest, so I get constant feedback. It's a wonderful way to live.

Inspirational moments aside, my main job is to offer students practical advice. I know all the ins and outs of our curriculum, so when kids get stuck I'm usually able to guide them to a better path. I recall one young man who was having a difficult time managing his workload as a business administration major. He was a sophomore when he came to see me. During our first meeting, he mentioned to me that he was interested in computers and thought that someday he could run his own computer store. That, however, required him to double major in computer science, and he didn't think he could handle it. So we sat down and mapped out a sensible plan. Once he saw it laid out in front of him, he went for it.

That young man got both degrees, and right after graduation he started working in a computer store down the street from campus. When that closed, he opened his own business. Pretty soon all the Loyola students were going over there to get their computers fixed. Every now and then he comes by campus and stops in to say hello. Those are the moments I live for as an educator.

I can never say this enough: I love being around young people. They keep me alive, healthy, and vibrant. They share their dreams and their fears. My interactions with those students are why I've never regretted not having children of my own. Sometimes they just want to hang out, despite my old-fashioned ideas. I'm sure it won't surprise you to learn that I'm not one for foul language. The worst I might say is "Oh, sugar!" which is what my sister-in-law does every time she gets mad. I'm sure our students use profanity, and I certainly don't judge them for that. Yet, I can't remember a single time when one of them said a curse word in my presence. They are so respectful.

The young people in college today give me so much hope because they are not afraid to speak up. Oftentimes they come into college knowing exactly what they want to do. That amazes me! There's always a big group that comes in undecided, and I tell them that's okay too. They can make those decisions in due time, and even after they've made some choices they can always change their minds.

At my age, it's a challenge to keep from becoming outdated. As far as I'm concerned, it's up to me to operate on their level more than the other way around. When they're playing music, I try to pay attention. When they speak, I listen very carefully. It's funny to me when they find new words to use. At least, they *think* the words are new, but I tell them we used those words back in the twenties. As the saying goes, there is nothing new under the sun.

Sometimes I'll join them for board games. I used to love playing board games with my family while growing up, as well as with the sisters I lived with all those years. Some of the students at Loyola recently invited me to play Yahtzee. I suggested Monopoly, but they said it takes too long. I told them they needed to refresh my memory on how to play Yahtzee, but that I'd love to join them—and try to win, of course.

I also connect with the students through our common love of sports. That always gives us something to talk about. I'm a big Chicago Bulls fan, and I got a huge thrill when Candace Parker came back to her hometown and helped the Chicago Sky win a WNBA championship in 2018. I'm also a big Chicago Bears fan. I've rooted for them especially hard these last few years. I feel like they need my sympathy now more than ever.

I have a wonderful view from my office in the first floor of the student center. I can see the students come and go all day. When it's lunchtime I have all the food I want just a few feet away. If I go into the cafeteria and see a student sitting alone, I try to engage them in conversation. Summers in Chicago are beautiful, but I miss the students when they're gone, and I'm happy when they return in the fall.

I think all of us are more appreciative of being at a special place like Loyola since the onset of the COVID pandemic. People understood what it felt like to be isolated from one another, and they didn't like it. When it was time to circulate again, they were more accepting of their neighbors. I think that the pandemic brought all of us closer together. I'm not saying we don't still have our differences, but I'd like to believe a new and more welcoming spirit emerged from this very trying period. Maybe I'm just being fanciful, but that is what I pray for.

I get asked a lot about my feelings on all the new technology. I'm not afraid to learn new things, unlike a lot of people my age. (Not that there are a lot of people my age.) As you have read, I am very active on email. I tell my students that email is better than text messaging. I'd rather they call than text me. Otherwise I'd be texting all day like a teenager. I prefer meeting face-to-face whenever possible. I know how to go online and check a student's class schedule, so if they want to meet, I can email some time slots I know they will be free.

The technology came in very handy during the pandemic. I couldn't attend my usual daily liturgical service in town, so instead I used my iPad to join a virtual mass at a church in Toronto. People got very confused when I told them I visited Toronto every morning.

I also write all my own emails. I don't have a secretary or use a voice-activated computer. I'm a pretty quick typist, although I recently developed what they call "trigger finger," where your finger gets locked in a bent position all of a sudden and you have to straighten it. That makes typing a little more time-consuming. I like my computer, although I don't like all those software updates when it seemed like things were working just fine. We've surely come a long way from having to put a nickel in the phone to make a call.

My experience with modern technology has not yet extended to social media. I think there is a lot of character defamation going on there. I do go on Twitter sometimes, but mostly to follow our teams or the *Loyola Phoenix*.

I see young people interacting with one another through their screens more than in person, and that troubles me. That's why I'm a big fan of group study sessions. That way, the students are talking directly to, and learning from, one another. You see them come alive. I love seeing them exchange ideas. It's very important for them to learn to tolerate one another, even when they disagree. *Especially* when they disagree. Nobody is going to agree on everything, but we still need to learn to respect one another.

Needless to say, it has been much more preferable to have the students back on campus. I've tried to do my part to help things return to normal. During a freshman orientation in the summer of 2022, I was having lunch with the orientation leaders and reminded them that they forgot to reinstate Christmas in July. We had to cancel it in 2020 because of COVID, and then they forgot to reinstate it the following year. This was a new group of student leaders, so they were unfamiliar with it. I explained to them that it's a Christmas party we have for administrative leaders on July 25. The school sets up a Christmas tree, serves hot cocoa and marshmallows to everyone, and then the students exchange gifts. I'm happy to report that Christmas in July was held once again that summer, and hopefully for every summer moving forward.

In recent years, and especially as a result of the pandemic, a lot of schools are doing away with using standardized tests for admission. I understand the reasons behind this, but I think it's a bad move. The standardized tests are an objective way of finding out how well the students work under pressure. The companies that produce these exams revise them every year to make sure they are both challenging and fair. I think it's especially helpful when the tests include a writing portion. That's a great way to tell how prepared a student is for college.

I recognize that it's harder for students of color and students from poor communities to score well, but I don't think the answer is to get rid of the tests. The answer is to improve their schools. It's also critical that colleges take into account a student's entire profile when deciding whether to admit someone. The test score should never be the be-all and end-all, but it can be helpful in determining a person's qualifications.

Even though we would like for every student to be admitted into every college, it can backfire if a student goes to a place where he or she is not ready to do the work. Many times the better option is to go to a community college for two years and then move on to a four-year school. But people don't want to wait for things, even if it means ending up in a better place.

～

I began this book by writing about the importance of setting aside quiet time for prayer and reflection. There is a widespread assumption that young people today don't want that. Yet, in our Information Commons building, we have a third floor where there's a rule against talking, and it's always crowded. The kids could study alone in their rooms if they wanted, but they would rather be with one another—and be quiet. I am glad to see they understand how powerful that can be.

When I encourage students to set aside quiet time, oftentimes they will answer, "I don't have time." My reply is always, "Yes, you do." We can do whatever we want with the time we have. It's up to us to decide whether we want to use that time profitably. Young people today expect things to happen very quickly. I'm not being critical, that's just the world they know. They make big plans and expect everybody else to jump when they make a telephone call. Eventually they get into the real world and find out that things don't always work like that.

I'm glad to hear that more and more young people are finding quiet time to meditate, or even go on retreats together. With all the devices and distractions, it's important that we make it a priority to give ourselves that kind of respite. It keeps us calm, it helps us be mentally healthy, and it brings us closer to God. That's all I could ever wish for them, and for you.

～

As I write these words, I am approaching my 103rd birthday. I could say I don't "feel" 103, but to be honest, there are some days that I do—in my body, anyway.

Life has slowed down to a somewhat manageable pace, but I wouldn't say that things are back to "normal." Nor do I want them to be! I love my life and all that comes with it. Just when I think that the whole Sister Jean craze is about to calm down, out of nowhere I'll get a request to do something or go somewhere, or make a video of some kind. The one thing I am careful about is autographing index cards that people send to me in the mail. I was advised not to do that because people sell them. So I usually send a signed picture instead. People are constantly coming by my office to ask for a picture. One night this past winter, I was waiting outside for my Uber near the bus stop. A student shouted from down the sidewalk, "Sister Jean, could I have your picture?" I told him, "If you think you can make it through the snow, go for it." Sometimes I think my life is just one big selfie.

I think people sense that I am a happy person and that I try to do as much good as I can. They can see how much I love these young people. Sometimes I'll get letters asking me to pray for someone they love. I got a letter from a man whose cousin was recovering from cancer, and he asked me to pray for him. I wrote him back and assured him that I would do just that.

I got an email recently from a fellow BVM sister who is living in Des Moines. She was watching one of our basketball games, and they showed me on TV. I hear the same things from my neighbors at The Clare. I never know when I'm being shown during a game. I just know how much I love being around those wonderful young men. All of our success paid off when we were invited to join the Atlantic

10 Conference for the start of the 2022–2023 season. This is a big step for us, but I'm sure that Drew and the gang are ready for it. I'm equally sure the other schools in the Missouri Valley Conference were happy to see us leave. I think they'd had enough of those pesky Ramblers.

One of my fears is that my mind will start to slip. I used to say to Father Garanzini, "If you hear me slipping, just say the word *Dubuque*, and I'll know what you mean." He never had to say it, thank God, and as far as I can tell, I still have all my marbles. I look forward to the day when I am strong enough to be out of this wheelchair. I've got too much work to do and too many places to go. And I've got plenty of comfortable shoes.

I am so fortunate that at this advanced stage of my life, I still go to bed every night with a smile on my face, gratitude in my heart, and love in my soul. As I nod off, I pat myself on the back for all the good things I've done that day, and then I thank God one more time for all the blessings He has bestowed on me during my first hundred years. I'm never quite certain what the morning will bring. All I know for sure is that I will wake up with purpose.

Epilogue

Life and Death

We shouldn't take ourselves so seriously, you know.

WHAT DO I HOPE people will get from reading this book?

I hope they'll learn good values. I've tried to let my life be guided by a certain set of principles. I'm not saying I've always lived up to them, but I've always tried. God didn't create us to be perfect. He created us to be human.

I hope this book will encourage people to play sports and to push their children to play them as well. Sports are the best teachers. Whether you're playing basketball, working behind a cash register, or performing duties as a doctor or lawyer, you have to be able to function as part of a team. The Ramblers, God bless them, show that every time they take the court.

I hope this book brings people joy and makes them chuckle once in a while. We shouldn't take ourselves so seriously, you know.

I also hope this book encourages young women to consider joining the BVM community. The motherhouse is still right there in Dubuque, ready to usher in the next generation of sisters. Unfortunately, our numbers have dwindled. There used to be several thousand of us, but now we're down to a few hundred, including the 180 or so retired sisters living on the Mount Carmel Bluffs campus.

I hope I've helped people understand that it's easy to do good if you want to do good. I know there are many service-oriented people out there. I hope the book will encourage them to try to be fully human and to show others that they're interested in them and sincerely care for them. If you can help someone, help them. We can't fix every problem, but we can always do the good that's in front of us.

I hope this book helps people become a little more forgiving—of themselves and others. We need forgiveness now more than ever. It's very hard for us to forgive because we don't like to be hurt. In those moments I think it's helpful to remind ourselves that we all make mistakes. If we can forgive those who have hurt us, it becomes easier to get past our pain. Anger and pain are difficult burdens to carry.

If people are feeling sad or angry or anxious, I hope this book will remind them to be grateful they're alive, to value their friends and family, and to stay positive as they chart a way forward. We all get discouraged. That's okay. God can show us to a better place, but it's up to us to ask Him and to trust Him. We all want big miracles, but there are lots of small miracles happening all around us every day, if we pay close enough attention.

I believe happiness is a choice. As hard as things get sometimes, we can still choose to be happy. And that choice can be contagious. We can make those around us a little happier if we choose to be happy ourselves.

Most of all, I hope this book brings people closer to God. God made us because He loves us. We should love Him for all He does for us. He created this wonderful, beautiful world. It's up to us to take care of it, and one another.

⸺

I remember being a little girl in Catholic school and first hearing about the judgment. I was scared because I thought it meant that all my sins would be announced to everybody, and all my friends and family would hear how bad I had been. I expressed this fear to my mother, and she told me that that's not what judgment means. "It's just going to be you and God," she said. "He'll decide what happens."

I do believe there's a judgment of some kind. Nobody knows, of course, but our God is a loving God. We all make mistakes. We all sin. We're all human. He knows that because He created us.

When people tell me they're afraid of dying, I tell them it's natural to have a little bit of fear in your heart. It's like when you're a little kid and you do something wrong and you don't want your parents to find out. God knows everything anyway.

As a sister, I don't officiate at funerals the way a pastor does, but I've attended more than my share. Families will often turn to me for words of comfort. It's very difficult, especially when I'm talking to a parent who has just lost a child. I encourage them to imagine the person who has passed walking around in heaven. I like to think that heaven is a place where if you're the new kid on the block, somebody will help you out. I don't know if that's theologically correct, but it's what I'd like to think is true.

Am I afraid of dying? Well, maybe a little. I can do the math. I know it could happen any day. When I wake up in the morning, I say,

"Thank you, God, for giving me another day." I check my arms and legs to make sure they're still working. Then I get going. I certainly never expected to live this long. When God wants me, He'll take me.

When that day does come—and it will come for us all—I hope I'm remembered as a loving person. I hope I'll be remembered for my kindness, for my love of my BVM community, for my love of teaching, my sports, my love for my community at Loyola and beyond. I hope people will think of me as someone who loved God and tried to do the things that God wanted. God called me, and I answered Him as best I could. I've loved my life, and I've enjoyed other people. I've never needed a lot of showy material possessions to be happy.

It's amazing to me that I would be in a position to publish a book like this. I'm held up as this extraordinary story, when in truth I am an ordinary person who has lived an ordinary life. I've never tried to be better than anyone. I've only tried to do the best I could at the things that make me happy. I've tried to encourage people to fortify their faith without telling them how to pray. I don't have all the answers, but I've tried to ask good questions, godly questions.

Sometimes I wonder, Why me? Why did I become so famous? Why was I blessed with this kind of platform so that I could spread God's grace and be an inspiration to others? I don't know the answer. There was a BVM sister named Sister Kathleen who was the chaplain of the Notre Dame football team, but she never got this kind of publicity even though the Irish were winning all of their games. I guess it's just one of those unknowns. We try so hard to make things happen. Sometimes we're successful, sometimes we're disappointed, and sometimes God just blows us away. We pray so hard and so often, and maybe we feel a little guilty about asking too much. And then God comes along, dispenses His miracles, and we realize that all along we were asking for too little.

Our God is a God of surprises. Some are unpleasant, but many are wonderful. Things will happen in life that we could never anticipate. God likes to keep us on our toes. He has blessed me with an amazing life full of love and purpose. I can't wait to see what He has in store for me next.

Acknowledgments

THIS BOOK TOOK A year to write, but it was a century in the making. Therefore, I would like to start by thanking my large and wonderful family for giving me life and teaching me how to live it. That includes my mother and father, brothers Ed and Ray and their children, and the extended Schmidt and Bowman families. Many of them are gone, but many more are still living and very much blessing my life, even though I don't get to see them these days as much as I'd like.

I am blessed to be a part of several faith communities that have brought me closer to God and taught me to spread His teachings and spirit to others. Thank you to the Sisters of Charity of the Blessed Virgin Mary, the Loyola community, and the Jesuit community.

I am grateful to have been taught the ways of the religious life by the leaders of the BVM Formation Team, Sister Mary Angelice Roach, Sister Majella Kent, and Sister Edwardetta Authur. May their memories be a blessing. Thank you also to the BVM sisters who guided me as members of the scholastic team at Mundelein

College: Sister Mary Hogan, Sister Joan Therese Scanlan, and Sister Frances Shea.

I was fortunate to be mentored by a group of principals who helped me mature from a wide-eyed novice into a seasoned teacher. Thank you Sister Mary Idus Slattery, Sister Mary Gilbert Reagan, Sister Mary Florence Casey, and Sister Mary Patrize Mulaney.

The presidents I served under at Mundelein had an enormous impact on my life and did amazing work in guiding that wonderful college. Sister Ann Ida Gannon was the first president I worked for there. She was way ahead of her time, and I still apply many things she taught me in my work today. The same can be said for the presidents who succeeded her, Sister Susan Rink, Sister Mary Breslin, and Sister Carolyn Farrell.

The Mundelein affiliation was very challenging, but Loyola continued to thrive due to the leadership of its Jesuit presidents under whom I have served: Friar Raymond Baumhart, Friar John Piderit, and Friar Michael Garanzini, as well as John Pelissero, JoAnn Rooney, and our current president, Dr. Mark C. Reed.

Thank you to the members of "Team Jean" who helped bring this book to fruition: agent David Black, HarperCollins Publisher and Acquiring Editor Matt Baugher, and co-author Seth Davis. I would like to add a special thanks to Seth's wife Melissa, his sons Zachary, Noah, and Gabriel, and his dogs Clarence and Sadie for generously loaning him to me for all those hours even though he was so busy with the basketball season. Thanks also to my HarperCollins teammates, John Andrade, Kara Brammer, Jennifer Moorman, T. J. Rathbun, and Kevin Smith.

I am blessed to work with one of the finest college athletics departments in the country, which is so ably led by our athletic director

Steve Watson. I am especially grateful to Bill Behrns, our assistant athletic director for communications, and his assistant, Ryan Haley, for handling all of my media requests and helping me to manage my schedule. Austin Hansen has done wonderful work as Loyola's director of video production.

Loyola senior associate athletics director Tom Hitcho has been my colleague for many years, and ever since I broke my hip, he has served as my de facto caretaker and wheelchair pusher. I am so grateful for his friendship, loyalty, and generosity. I don't know what I would do without him.

Thank you to the communities that give me so much love and support: the Caregiver Group, the Loyola Medical Group, the Prayer Group, the Clare SMILE Group, and the Mundelein graduates.

The basketball coaches at Loyola have welcomed me into their programs with open arms and given this old nun a sense of purpose that I cherish. I will be forever grateful to Ken Burmeister, Larry Farmer, Jim Whitesell, Porter Moser, and Drew Valentine.

I wish I could thank by name every student I have taught at the six schools where I have worked. Their friendship and the memories I have from teaching them sustain me to this day. I am also grateful for so many friends and colleagues who have stayed in touch and visited with me for so many years. If I tried to list all of them here, I would have to write another book. (Say, that's not a bad idea!) Thanks to Mark Adams, Cindy Bertram, Friar Mark Bosco, Margaret Callahan, Susan Cibulskis, Dawn Collins, Friar Justin Daffron, Friar Patrick Dorsey, Sister Dorothy Dwight, Dr. Angela Frank, Sister Margaret Geraghty, Rebecca Grim, Phil Hale, Jo Beth Halpin, Marilee Halpin, Friar Scott Hendrickson, Juan Helden, Cookie Krupa, Joe Lunardi, Mary Ann McGinley, Sister Mary Fran McLaughlin, Jane Neufeld,

Acknowledgments

Cathy O'Sullivan, Friar Jerry Oberbeck, Betty Parkinson, Friar Jim Prehn, Lisa Reitner, Sister Sandra Rodmeyer, Patrick Schulz, Janet Sisler, Beccy Sullivan, Dr. Louis Tenta, Ramiza Vulic, Anne Wicker, and Sister Mary Ann Zollman. My apologies to those friends whom I did not mention.

Thank you to all the amazing young men who have played basketball for Loyola during my tenure as team chaplain. I can't name one without naming all of them, so I'll just acknowledge them as a group and let them know how much they mean to me. I trust they will always treasure the memories and life lessons they acquired while playing for the Ramblers. And I hope they will always remember the importance of boxing out.

Oftentimes when I am asked to give a prayer, I close by thanking "the God of all of us." That is how I like to think of Him. We all imagine God a different way and refer to Him with different names, but that's okay. The important thing is to believe in God and do your best to follow His teachings and live a good life. So my final thank you is to the God of all of us. May He continue to bless us with His strength, wisdom, guidance, and grace.

About the Authors

SISTER JEAN DOLORES SCHMIDT IS a religious sister of the Sisters of Charity of the Blessed Virgin Mary. She has spent her entire adult life working as a teacher, administrator, and volunteer, first at elementary and grade schools in Chicago and Los Angeles, and later at Mundelein College and Loyola University. Since 1994, Sister Jean, as she is known, has served as team chaplain for Loyola's men's basketball team. She gained national—and international—fame in 2018 when the Ramblers went on a Cinderella run to the Final Four. Sister Jean has been a household name ever since. In August 2022 Sister Jean celebrated her 103rd birthday.

SETH DAVIS is an award-winning college basketball studio analyst for CBS Sports and a senior writer for college basketball at *The Athletic*. Since 2004 he has been a mainstay of CBS and Turner Sports coverage of the NCAA tournament. Seth is the author of eight books, including the *New York Times* bestsellers *Wooden: A Coach's Life* and *When March Went Mad: The Game That Transformed*

Basketball; the memoir *Equinunk, Tell Your Story: My Return to Summer Camp*; and *The Soccer Prince*, a novel for middle school readers. He lives in Los Angeles with his wife, Melissa, their sons, Zachary, Noah, and Gabriel, and their Goldendoodles, Clarence and Sadie.